D. J. SMITH

Discovering
Horse-drawn Caravans

SHIRE PUBLICATIONS LTD

Contents

ACKNOWLEDGEMENTS

The author and publishers acknowledge with gratitude the help of the following in the preparation of this book: George L. Shearer, Curator of the Hereford and Worcester County Museum; Edward Cripps, Conservation and Technical Services Officer, Hereford and Worcester County Museum; the Curator and staff of the Museum of English Rural Life; M. Brindley; B. B. Murdock; K. Bennett; Mrs J. M. Webb; J. Windfall; Lesley Watkinson; the Irish National Tourist Board. Figure 6 is reproduced by kind permission of the Caravan Club.

Cover photograph. A Burton caravan built about 1900 (Lesley Watkinson).

First published 1981. Number 258 in the Discovering series. ISBN 0 85263 565 6.

Set in 9 on 9 point Times Roman and printed in Great Britain by Hunt Barnard Printing Ltd, Aylesbury.

1. Introduction

The caravan is essentially a mobile home or lodging, associated by the average person with the roving life of gypsies and other travellers. Yet it is only in comparatively modern times that gypsies have possessed living vans (vardos) and then only in parts of the world where they became prosperous. The caravan may have been so called because it often travelled in convoys or caravans, or the word may be a mispronunciation of the Persian *karwan*, which was a long-distance travelling coach of the Middle East.

The forerunner of the caravan was a roughly made cart or wagon used by nomadic tribesmen from the heartland of central Asia – a development almost as old as the wheel. Like some of the gypsy caravans, they were little more than tents or tilts fitted above a wheeled platform, yet affording greater security than bivouacs at ground level. Such vehicles offered both a domicile and a place of storage, accompanying nomads on their historic treks over the Eurasian landmass. Many such people finally settled on the plains of eastern Europe, along the course of the lower Danube, being the Magyar ancestors of the Hungarian nation. The traditions of wagon building were widely cherished and developed among the Magyars and their modern descendants. Some of the earliest recognisable living vans in Europe may have been used on the Hungarian plains (Puszta), as were many other varieties of coach, cart and wagon.

The use of caravans was not restricted to herdsmen of the plains. Many were also used by itinerant craftsmen such as potters, tinkers and harnessmakers, serving a dual purpose as living quarters and mobile workshop. They were widely used by showmen and entertainers, especially on a seasonal basis, and also, in later years, by surveyors, engineers and contractors working some distance from their home base. Missionaries of several Christian sects and denominations frequently used caravans, especially during the 1890s and 1900s, while in America there were even chapels on wheels or 'gospel wagons', suitable for conducting full-length services and fitted with pipe organs.

Pleasure caravans first appeared during the second half of the nineteenth century and were often large vehicles drawn by pairs or teams of horses, although there were some that could be towed to and from the camp site but were taken for the greater part of their journey by railway on flat wagons or carriage trucks. Until the period between the world wars and the era of popular motoring, caravanning was a pastime for wealthy people with ample funds and leisure. It was not until the early 1930s that many ordinary folk began to invest in trailer caravans as an alternative to family hotels and boarding houses for a cheaper but less restrictive holiday.

Many of the larger trailers have found their way to permanent sites, jacked up and losing their identity as vehicles, although since the late 1960s there has been a revival of horse caravanning in several countries, especially the west of Ireland, where large towns are few and far apart, and motor traffic less troublesome to horses.

Most gypsies and travelling folk now tour the high roads and byways in motor-drawn trailers, but a few (up to six per cent) still retain horses. It was among the gypsies that some of the more interesting horse-drawn caravans developed, and a description of these forms the main content of this book.

It has been said that the future pattern of life may increasingly depend on temporary or even mobile dwellings, with fewer permanent homes. At least ninety thousand people in Britain are known to live permanently in mobile homes of one kind or another, while many more live on semi-permanent camp sites, only a few of whom are of gypsy blood.

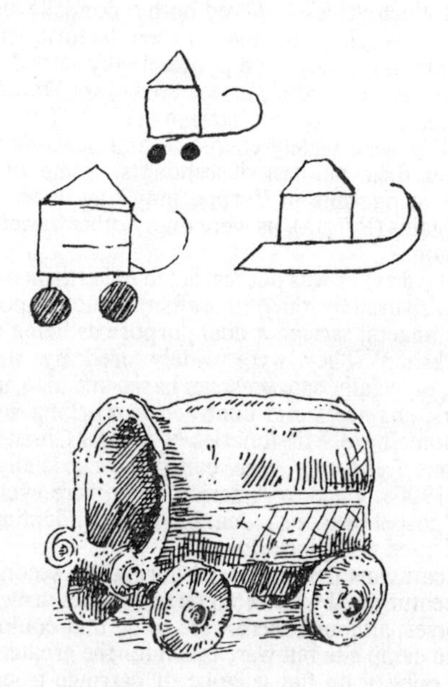

1. Ancient representations of early forms of caravan: (top left) early pictographic symbols from Uruk, Mesopotamia, c 3000 BC; (top right) caravan developed from a slide or sledge, early Mesopotamia; (bottom) clay model of early covered wagon from Tepe Gawra, Mesopotamia.

2. Origins and development

The first caravan was descended from a covered wagon, which may have been little more than a sledge or slide, eventually fitted with disc wheels or rounded sections hacked from the near-circular trunk of a tree. Illustrations of such vehicles have been scratched or engraved on record tablets found in the temple of Uruk, Mesopotamia, dating back to 3000 BC. These are pictorial symbols rather than true illustrations but show a gable-like roof above a typical square framework. The exact purpose of these vehicles is not recorded although it may be assumed that such types were similar to covered carts used by the nomads of central Asia, some of which may have penetrated to the Near and Middle East through passes of the Hindu Kush and the mountains of the Caucasus.

In recent years clay models were unearthed at Tepe Gawra in Mesopotamia, suggesting a definite link between the Fertile Crescent and the steppes of central Asia or southern Siberia, beyond the Caspian Sea. These closely resembled the covered wagon of American pioneers used in their exploration and conquest of the far west. E. A. Speiser, who excavated these artifacts, dates such vehicles to the middle of the third millennium BC. Other covered wagons of this period are believed to have been used for various religious or cult ceremonies.

The car-temples of Juggernaut, some over 30 feet (9 m) high and larger than the average house, may be described as a form of caravan, these being a feature of Hindu culture – in which priests lived and worshipped – from almost prehistoric times. Many scholars attribute the invention of both the wheel and the wagon to ancient India, but the Chinese lay equal claim to these inventions, which number among the most significant in the later development of mankind. It is certain that carts and chariots played an important part in the rise of Chinese civilisation for both warlike and peaceful purposes. Shafts, as opposed to the centre pole and neck yoke, appear to have been first used in China and central Asia, taken westwards by nomadic migrations during the dark ages. European countries and lands bordering the Mediterranean used spans of oxen, especially for heavy draught, over a considerable period, while oriental cultures east of the Caspian and north of the Himalayas made greater use of single beasts of burden between a pair of shafts or thills.

There is very little difference between the appearance and purpose of certain caravans and covered wagons. Those that developed in Europe during the late middle ages were a form of travelling hotel for long or short journeys, at seasons of the year when the few roads or rutted tracks were still usable. It later became customary, however, to halt at wayside inns to change

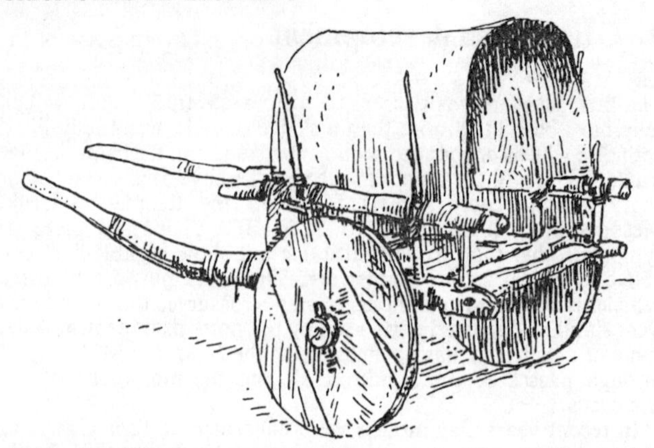

2. Tilted cart from western China, similar to those used in central Asia by nomadic herdsmen.

horses and allow the passengers time to recover. Long periods spent in a clumsy vehicle without brakes or springs were far from being a pleasure jaunt or means of relaxation. In Germany and other parts of central Europe the lumbering wagons used to carry military stores in time of war frequently served as caravans for soldiers and their families or camp followers, both on foreign and home service. At night they would be drawn into a defensive circle, as with the wagon trains in North America, used as a primitive defence work on the field of battle or as a mobile town and headquarters, known as a *wagenburg*. Towards the end of the fifteenth century the deployment of these baggage or living wagons played an important role in military tactics. In central and eastern Europe towns were often further apart than in the countries bordering the North Sea and Mediterranean. The long-distance traveller or soldier campaigning in eastern Europe was thus more dependent on a mobile home or defence system than his counterparts further west and south.

The britschka and the dormeuse, both large travelling carriages of the late eighteenth and early nineteenth centuries, were essentially of eastern European origins. The occupants could spend the night in them while on journeys where other accommodation was either dubious or non-existent. Carriage servants had to huddle on the rear or rumble seat, under hood and apron, but the passenger compartment could be fitted out with beds – not unlike the *carruca dormitoria* or sleeping carriage of the Roman Empire. At one period the britschka was greatly favoured by travelling diplomats, also by those exploring new territory with the aim of planning roads, railways or canal systems. I. K. Brunel spent several weeks in a britschka while surveying the main line of the Great Western Railway between Bristol and London.

The covered wagon of North America originated as a general purpose vehicle from the Conestoga Valley, Pennsylvania, adapted for overland treks by settlers of Teutonic descent. They were used, to a lesser extent, by the British and Dutch, but mainly by German colonists or the so-called Pennsylvanian Dutch, guided perhaps by ancestral memories of the *wagenburg* or defensive circle of living wagons, which also proved successful in their encounters with hostile redskins.

The main difference between covered wagon and caravan lay in the length and permanence of their period of use. While the caravan was either a permanent dwelling or holiday home for fixed periods of the year, a covered wagon was merely a temporary abode for a journey of limited duration, although in the case of many early settlers and pioneers it was a journey lasting many months.

While large-wheeled vehicles could be used on plain or prairie and in areas where there were good roads, they were unsuitable in countries such as England between the end of the Roman occupation and the seventeenth century. Although the greater part of England was cultivated and in private ownership during this period, roadmaking was either discouraged or neglected, unstinted communications between centres being contrary to the inward looking and self-contained attitude of a feudal or near-feudal

3. Conestoga wagon, North America, eighteenth and nineteenth centuries.

society. Most traffic until the eighteenth century and the founding of a turnpike system was limited to rivers and coastwise trade, eventually supplemented by navigation canals. It was not until the second half of the eighteenth century that trunk roads returned to full use, although suffering a further period of neglect between the almost total domination of the railways from the late 1850s to the repeal of the Road Locomotives Act thirty years later.

Until the establishment of turnpikes the roads of Britain were quagmires in winter and scored with iron-hard ruts in summer, making passage over them impossible except for heavier types of vehicle with broad tyres. The gypsies and other travellers of those days would have found the living van or vardo more an embarrassment than an asset and were mainly dependent on pedestrian wanderings, although some may have had pack ponies or light two-wheeled carts – either handcarts or horse-drawn vehicles. Poor and solitary gypsies slept in hedges, haystacks or ruined buildings, as many of their European counterparts were likely to do until comparatively modern times. Those with larger families or greater substance would eventually have had their own tents, some of which may have been carried on ponies or asses but also mounted on small carts, although essentially demountable until the 1820s or 1830s. Not until the mid nineteenth century did gypsies live extensively in vans or vardos, while the finest and most typical caravans date from the second half of the century, becoming recognisable types that flourished until the 1930s.

The geographical and racial descent of true gypsies or Romany people is still veiled in mystery, although tribes and clans of their lineage wandered the trade routes and byways of three continents for many centuries. In some parts of Asia, southern Europe and North Africa, however, they also established themselves as cave dwellers or constructed primitive huts in tribal communities. It was only in Britain, France and Germany that large numbers were ever wealthy or enterprising enough to afford living vans and horses to pull them. This may have been because these countries were more advanced and prosperous at the time when comfortable and compact living vans first came into widespread use, with better roads and general conditions for all sections of the community. In countries that were rich and progressive even the poor were better off than their counterparts in more backward areas.

Certain types of living van or wagon (more frequently known as vans) may have been on the roads of England since the late seventeenth century, but these were the makeshift primitive vehicles of such travellers as mountebanks, market hucksters and broom or basket makers, selling their wares in villages and market towns. At one time there may well have been more pedlars and tinkers in living vans than true gypsies, and one of the Romany characters in *Lavengro* by George Borrow, a semi-autobiographical work, relates how she 'hated all basketmakers and folk living in caravans'. In *Wild Wales*, the account of a walking tour during the early 1850s, George Borrow describes his meeting with 'Captain' Jack Bosvile, a half gypsy (Posh Rat) and one of the tinker clan, also famed as a bare-knuckle fighter. Bosvile, apparently known to Borrow at an earlier stage of his career, was travelling through South Wales in what was described as a 'wooden house on wheels drawn by two horses coming down the hill towards me'.

The circus proprietor George Sanger, writing in his autobiographical *Seventy Years a Showman*, records how his father, after honourable discharge from the Royal Navy in 1805, constructed his own living van before taking to the roads, first as a showman and later as a huckster. This van was made of sheet iron on a wooden framework, spacious and comfortable during a temperate period, but far too hot in summer and cold in the depths of winter.

The original caravan of an improved type, apart from the tented carts or makeshift efforts of tinkers and pedlars, was constructed to professional standards by a Frenchman of Venetian origins named Antoine Franconi (1738–1836). During his long and eventful life Franconi was by turn a bullfighter, soldier of fortune, trick rider and horse trainer, but above all a doyen of the travelling circus. While Astley of London is credited with the first modern circus held in a sawdust ring, this was a static show remaining on one site, the Astley Amphitheatre. Franconi was proprietor of a tenting show that moved from town to town throughout Europe and the Near East, rarely staying for more than a day or so on each pitch. He eventually designed and occupied a large caravan with two separate rooms and a rear gallery or balcony, known as a *voiture nomad*, in which he also spent the greater part of his retirement. The appearance of this vehicle coincided with the great programme of road building initiated by the first Napoleon, but it may have been another twenty years before such vehicles crossed the English Channel. The first authentic sketch or picture of a caravan in England dates back to about 1840.

The original cooking and heating stove, first used in French vehicles, was the invention of Count Rumford (1753–1814), a man of universal genius who, although a poverty-stricken orphan from the American colonies, became eminent as a soldier, scientist, author and inventor. He lived both in France and in Bavaria, where he became a minister of state and was awarded a title of the Holy Roman Empire, Rumford being the name of the settlement in New Hampshire (later renamed Concord) where the family of his first wife originally settled. Much of his later work was directed towards the alleviation of poverty and its miseries, of which he considered a simple and economic stove, suitable for either cottager or van dweller, one of the first necessities.

The living vans of showmen, traders and craft workers all came before those of gypsies, very few of the Romany people having much more than a tilted cart before the 1850s. Those used by contractors and workmen were in a different category again, although widely advertised towards the end of the century in trade journals and the catalogues of commercial cart and wagon builders. Croskills of Beverley in Humberside specialised in the heavier types of horse-drawn vehicle, building large numbers of so called sleeping vans for both contractors and county or district councils. These were squarish upright vehicles with no pretensions of outward beauty, often with a well floor and a clerestory roof for extra headroom. Some would be further utilised as offices and store rooms but they usually had a cooking stove and a side bunk, occupied by a foreman in charge of a public enterprise, such as road mending or drainage work, some distance from the nearest town. A similar type of mobile office, sometimes with living accommodation, was used by the Royal Engineers for field duties; it could double as a mobile studio and darkroom for military photographers or for lithographic map printing. From the 1900s until the Second World War a popular contractor's van was designed for steam roller attendants and widely used after the more important roads, with the rapid development of motor traffic, were resurfaced with tarmacadam. This was pulled by a single horse between shafts but led on foot, following steam roller, water cart, tar boiler, tar van and a so called heavy traction wagon (attached to the steam roller itself) for coal and stores. Such vans were usually dead-axle or unsprung, but with screw-down brakes operated by a hand wheel. When not in use they were often left on a roadside verge, windows shuttered and half door (similar to a stable door) padlocked, to be collected when needed. Permission was often granted to park the contractor's or council-owned van in a farmer's rickyard, where it might be sheltered and less in the way of other road users, especially when cattle were still driven to market on the hoof using grass verges for rest and grazing.

Sleeping vans with both wooden and iron wheels, usually equirotal (the same size back and front), were also used by men on farm contract work, usually steam ploughing and threshing on the larger holdings of the eastern counties. The shepherd's hut or hut on wheels, in which he spent many nights away from home at lambing time, was also a form of rustic caravan, drawn from place to place by a farm horse. It was often roughly constructed from scrap wood and iron, with wheels taken from unwanted farm vehicles or implements, although a few were made to order or converted from old horse buses by the local joiner and wheelwright. Some living vans used by herdsmen and shepherds in such countries as the United States of America, Australia and New Zealand were more elaborate and nearer the ideal of a true caravan.

Missonary vans were used by a wide range of sects, especially

4. Contractor's van, 1912.

5. Missionary van, c 1902.

nonconformists and the Salvation Army. In the latter case they may have doubled as canteens or soup kitchens, distributing comforts in distressed areas suffering from prolonged strikes or unemployment. Those used by evangelical missions were usually manned by two or three clergymen or by an ordained minister and his lay assistants, all of whom might take turns to preach from the front porch of the van at open-air meetings and in market places, especially from the 1890s until the early 1920s.

The first horse-drawn caravan designed strictly for pleasure and recreation was the brainchild of Dr Gordon Stables, appearing in 1886 and now preserved at Bristol Industrial Museum. This was built by the Bristol Carriage and Waggon Works Limited, a firm noted for making delivery vans of the railway cartage service and Pullman cars for express trains in both Europe and America. Dr Stables was a retired naval officer and pioneer cyclist who also qualified as a medical doctor and wrote adventure books for boys. During the 1880s a number of wealthy people had discovered the joys of touring the English countryside and were buying second-hand gypsy caravans, a fad that might last a few seasons, similar to the adventures of Mr Toad in *The Wind in the Willows*. Dr Stables took the matter seriously enough to design his own living van and later wrote an entertaining book on the subject, which marked the beginning of an era. This was *The Cruise of the Land Yacht Wanderer*, describing how he came to take an interest in caravans, seemingly after a road accident when he was invited by a friendly van dweller to rest and recuperate in his nearby vardo. Dr Stables soon came to admire the comfort and convenience of a mobile home, far superior, in his opinion, to long-distance cycling or hiking, for he was a fanatic for overland travel and the outdoor life. He realised that one of the best ways of seeing the countryside was by road, although at a leisurely pace and not always keeping to the beaten (tourist) tracks. Being a rich man and conscious of his status in life, he rejected the idea of ordering a van from the usual makers, perhaps discouraged, although half amused, by ill spelt letters from one of them claiming that 'is yard could bild a waggon as ill carry you anywheres' and deliver the same with '1 orse for eity pounds'. The *Wanderer* weighed 30 hundredweight (1,500 kg) tare and just under 2 tons (2,000 kg) loaded with furniture and stores. Leading dimensions were 20 feet by 6 feet by 11 feet (6.10 m by 1.83 m by 3.35 m). It was drawn by a pair of horses in the care of a professional coachman, acting as both driver and groom. Dr Stables was also accompanied by his valet or gentleman's gentleman. The valet would ride ahead of the van on a tricycle, booking accommodation at country inns and farmhouses, also arranging stabling and fodder for the horses. Dr Stables usually slept in the van while this was parked in a private yard or enclosure, his coachman-groom sleeping in hotel rooms or other lodgings. His valet, to be close at hand, slept on a cork mattress in the kitchen.

Wanderer was built of the best materials throughout, with mahogany panelling, being twice the weight and length of an ordinary vardo. It cost over £300 to construct.

Caravanning eventually became an agreeable pastime for people of all classes, with varying degrees of comfort and luxury. It had a particular attraction for artists, bohemians and the less conventional (even if well heeled) sections of society. It was a way of life that greatly appealed to Augustus John, the society portrait painter, Lady Eleanor Smith, the novelist daughter of Lord Birkenhead, and the Royal Academicians Harold and Dame Laura Knight. After the First World War many pleasure caravans were motorised, while small trailer vans were manufactured for towing behind saloon cars. A few traditional vans, deprived of wheels and undergear, were even mounted on the rear platforms of steam wagons or motor lorries.

The Caravan Club, which did so much for amateurs and leisure seekers in this sphere, was founded by Harris J. Stone in 1907. Mr Stone was the friend and disciple of Dr Stables, writing widely on the subjects of caravanning and camping. Many of the early enthusiasts built their own vans or bought them second-hand from professional travellers, while other vans were available to club members, rented on a weekly basis in a modest price range from £2 to £9 or £10. There were usually fifty caravans on hire at one time, during the summer season. Such vans, either hired or privately owned, had nameplates over the doorways with romantic titles such as *Pegasus, Bird of Dawning, Tally Ho* or *Romany Maid*. The vans of showmen often had the owner's name on the centre of the door, above the letter box.

A passage from *The Wind in the Willows* describes the type of van that would appeal to a wealthy amateur about 1900. The colour, in particular, would not have been liked by gypsies or other professional travellers, who preferred strong reds and greens. 'He led the way to the stable yard accordingly . . . and there, drawn out of the coach-house into the open, they saw a gypsy caravan, shining with newness, painted a canary-yellow picked out with green, and red wheels ... It was indeed very compact and comfortable. Little sleeping-bunks – a little table that folded against the wall – a cooking stove, lockers, bookshelves, a birdcage with a bird in it; and pots, pans, jugs and kettles of every size and variety.'

6. The 'Wanderer', built in 1886 by the Bristol Carriage and Waggon Works for Dr Gordon Stables, was the first horse-drawn caravan designed for pleasure touring.

3. Types of caravan

Although caravans were not widely used by gypsies until the mid nineteenth century, by the 1880s several different types could be recognised that were almost exclusive to them. By this time, also, gypsies in all parts of Britain had become the greatest users of mobile homes, retaining this pre-eminence for the next sixty years. The popularity of the gypsy caravan was almost as short-lived as that of the improved mail or stage coach, but during its brief reign it became almost as successful in capturing the public imagination – the caravan *per se*, which automatically springs to mind when considering such vehicles. For this reason, dealing with horse-drawn caravans in greater detail, the gypsy van has been given precedence.

Although the word *gypsy* is accurate as a term in law to describe a nomadic person without fixed address or occupation, it was not always liked by the people so styled. Although accepting *gypsy* as a matter of simple convenience most people in this category called themselves *Romanies*, while those who lived with them and followed their ways were *Romany Ryes*; the half-breeds were *Posh Rats*, while those with quarter blood or less were *Didikais*. The non-gypsy of any race was a *Gorgio*. Gypsies are thought to have originated in northern India many centuries ago, but are now widely distributed in all continents. They came to Europe via the Middle East and Egypt, where some of their race were settled for a considerable time (or wandering in that area), taking the name *Egyptian* or people of Egypt, of which *gyptian* and later *gypsy* are corruptions. While the first European gypsies were travelling in Greece and Macedonia during the eighth century AD, they only came to Britain in large numbers during the sixteenth century,

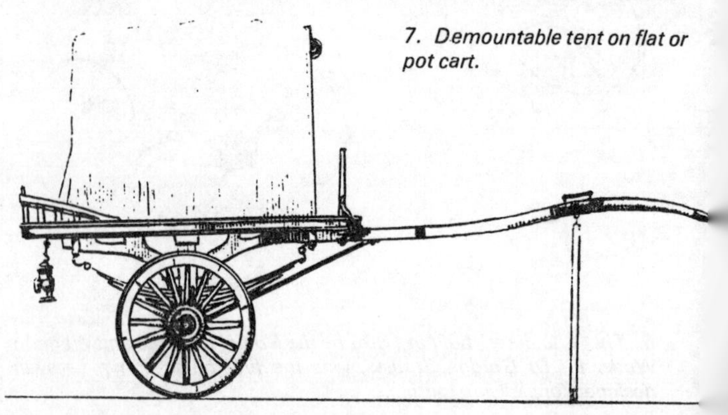

7. Demountable tent on flat or pot cart.

being established much earlier in the Balkans, central Europe, Russia and Spain. A few were persuaded to settle and took to farming on a small scale but the majority preferred the nomadic life, following such trades as pot mending, harness repairing, pegmaking and fortune telling (*dukkeripen*), while others lived by poaching and seasonal work, especially harvesting, hop and fruit picking. In Britain the wealthiest and those eventually owning the best caravans were the horse dealers, later becoming scrap metal merchants as horses were less widely needed. Gypsies were better tolerated by the Celtic peoples of Scotland, Wales and Ireland than in England. The English, especially the middle classes, tended to be more insular and suspicious of strangers in their midst, while the sight of idle or independent persons often aroused a feeling of mingled envy and contempt among those forced to work long hours for low wages.

Pot carts

The first identifiable vehicle adopted by gypsies as a mobile dwelling was the pot cart, perhaps thirty years or more after it had been discovered by other travellers. This was originally a two-wheeled vehicle, which is the true definition of a cart. A later and larger version was technically a wagon or van but always known to travellers as the 'four-wheeled pot cart'. Both vehicles consisted of a platform covered by a bow-shaped canvas tilt drawn over hoops. When the two-wheeled version was needed as a sleeping compartment the shafts were supported by propsticks or struts, let down on each side. These vehicles were descended from a potter's cart used not so much by makers of pots but by hucksters (both gypsies and non-gypsies) selling pottery seconds and cheap earthenware from door to door or in open markets, using the cart as a makeshift stall. Some pot carts were also known as flat carts, closely resembling the Bradford cart, the framework of four or more semicircular hoops boarded up to the height of three horizontal planks. Later versions were often mounted on sideways leaf springs of the semi-elliptical type, although sometimes with a combination of two sideways springs and a single set of cross springs. Shafts were either straight or slightly curved towards the ends.

The **two-wheeled pot cart** was not a true caravan and is more correctly termed a sleeping cart. It was of light construction with the platform almost square, little more than 6 feet (1.83 m) long, but sometimes slightly raised towards the rear end with spindles and brackets, not unlike a costermonger's cart or fruit barrow. The framework of later types tended to be barrel-shaped with a slight outward bulge of the hoops. The canvas covering could be rolled down at the back, so that the vehicle was usually entered through the front, between the shafts. Some carts were entirely boarded up at the back with a side depth of matchboarding about 2 feet

(610 mm) high. A rear window was not unknown and most carts had weather-proofed canvas curtains at the front. When the propsticks were not used on a stationary vehicle the shafts were frequently raised on boulders or the crossbars of a gate or thrust into a bush or hedge. One of the main assets of the pot cart was its lightness and manoeuvrability, taking up the minimum space on a grass verge or in a side lane. Some wheels, especially on the later types, had as many as sixteen spokes.

The **four-wheeled pot cart** was a light wagon, usually equirotal or near-equirotal. It was boat-shaped with fairly shallow side planks or panelling. Like some of the larger vans or vardos (*vardo* or *wardo* was the Romany name for a caravan), it had a pan box and cratch or shelf for extra storage at the rear end. The pan box usually fitted under and between the rear wheels.

While most had removable tops (hoops) and canvas tilts or covers, some versions had a *Yorkshire accommodation top*, this being a crosswise mounted bed box at the fore end of the vehicle, fitted with semicircular, canvas-covered hoops on both sides and supported on short legs that held it in position. The hoops were about 4 feet to 4 feet 6 inches (1,220 to 1,370 mm) high in the centre, while the canvas covering was often little more than a plain wagon or rick sheet. The bed or bed box was normally 6 feet by 3 feet 10 inches (1,830 to 1,170 mm) with vertical side boards about 10 inches (250 mm) high all round. When mounted in a crosswise position there was a slight overlap on either side. Such beds were also used, to a lesser extent, on two-wheeled pot carts. When the cart was used for other purposes, such as hawking, the top would be removed or dismantled.

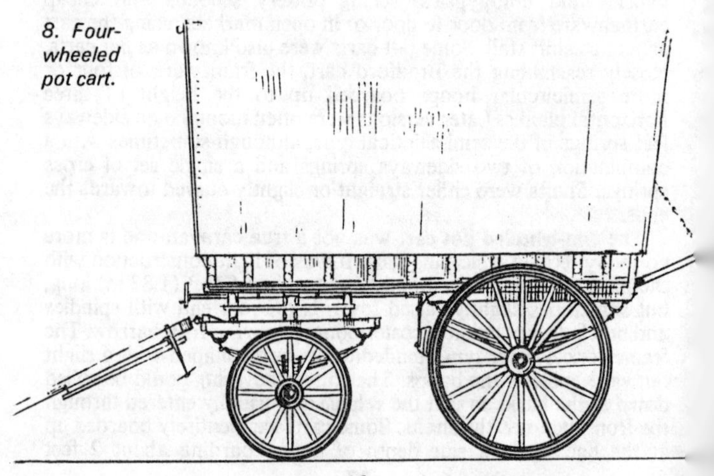

8. Four-wheeled pot cart.

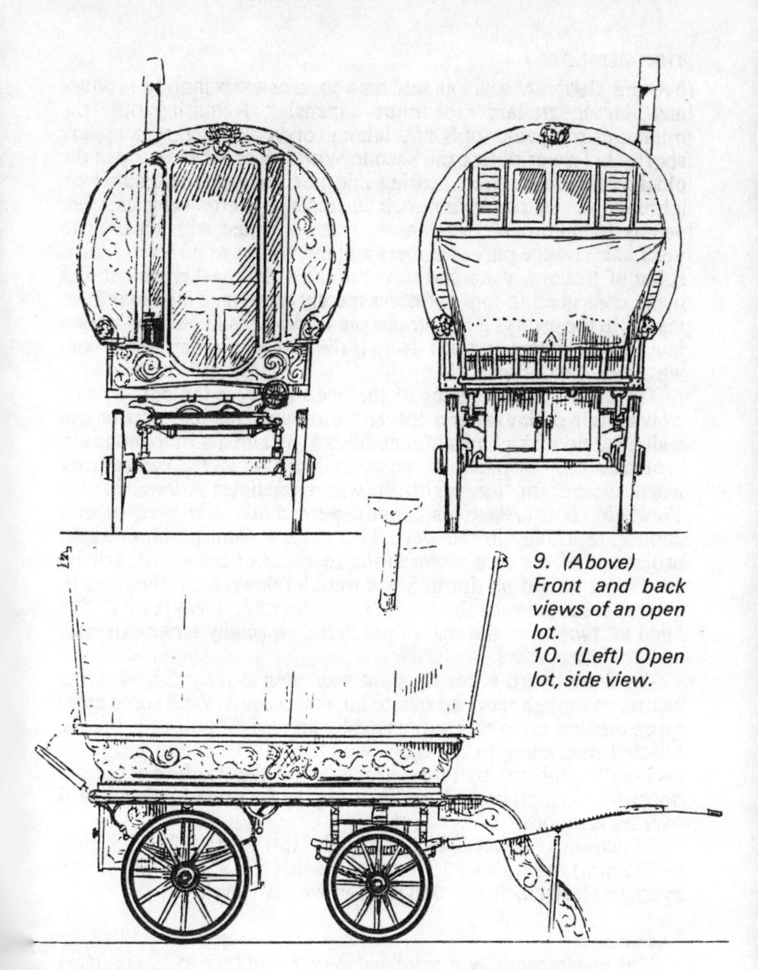

9. *(Above) Front and back views of an open lot.*
10. *(Left) Open lot, side view.*

The open lot

This type is still being made in limited numbers, although predating in style many of the larger and more elaborate vans of both gypsies and showmen. It is in direct line of descent from the pot carts and survives because it is easy to construct and maintain. Many of this type were enlarged versions of the four-wheeled pot cart or later bow top, converted from surplus light drays and the once familiar trolleys or rulleys owned by dealers and tradesmen. Any flat open vehicle would be suitable for conversion, frequently undertaken by the new owner – a person skilful with his hands but needing elaborate tools as well as a yard or workshop to produce anything much larger or more expensive. Requiring only the minimum of space, tools and labour, open lots began to appear shortly before or during the Second World War, when many of the older van builders were retiring and few younger men, either on national service or turning their interests to motor vehicles, were willing to take over from them. This coincided with an urge to mechanise on the part of traders and merchants at all levels, and a spate of trolleys, vans and drays flooded the market, sometimes being consigned to mass bonfires merely to salvage metalwork for resale. In those days a light trade van or dray could be bought for a few pounds, perhaps given away if the owner of a new motor van was in a generous mood.

The chief characteristics of the open lot were the bow-shaped canvas tops on hoops or a curved framework, the rear part or end wall filled up with planks of matchboarding and a semi-open front, protected only or partly by curtains, laced down the centre front when closed for the night. It was sometimes known as the *Yorkshire bow* because so many were made and used in that county, especially in the west. There was a front porch or slight projection of the roof towards the rear end of the shafts, but no footboard or end platform. Steps were let down from the front to ground level, between the shafts, when the vehicle was resting. The open lot took over the role of pot carts, especially among the less well-to-do travellers.

The front board of the open lot was often slightly dipped in the centre, as though scooped out, to improve access. With some early types the first hoop was supported by an upright pole or prop, the lowered part being to the right on entering. The centre prop was eventually replaced by two uprights about the width of a normal doorway, terminating above in a highly decorated crownboard over the entrance.

Dimensions: 9 feet 3 inches (2,819 mm) long; 5 feet 2 inches (1,575 mm) wide; about 15 hundredweight (762 kg) tare weight; on average 3 feet 4 inches (1,016 mm) above road level.

The bow top

This was essentially a small ledge-type van (not to be confused with the larger and more elaborate ledge van or 'cottage on wheels'), with low side panels and a pronounced overhang of the upperwork. The well rounded bow-shaped top fitted on to a framework similar to that of the open lot, members being of steam-bent ash wood. Hoops or bows were eight in number, with 15 inches (381 mm) between centres, on a typical van. Numerous versions of this type were made in Yorkshire, Lincolnshire, the Midlands and even Scotland (Falkirk), with sub-types known as *bell, barrel* and *square top*, mainly depending on the external shapes of the framework. There was an oblong rear window and

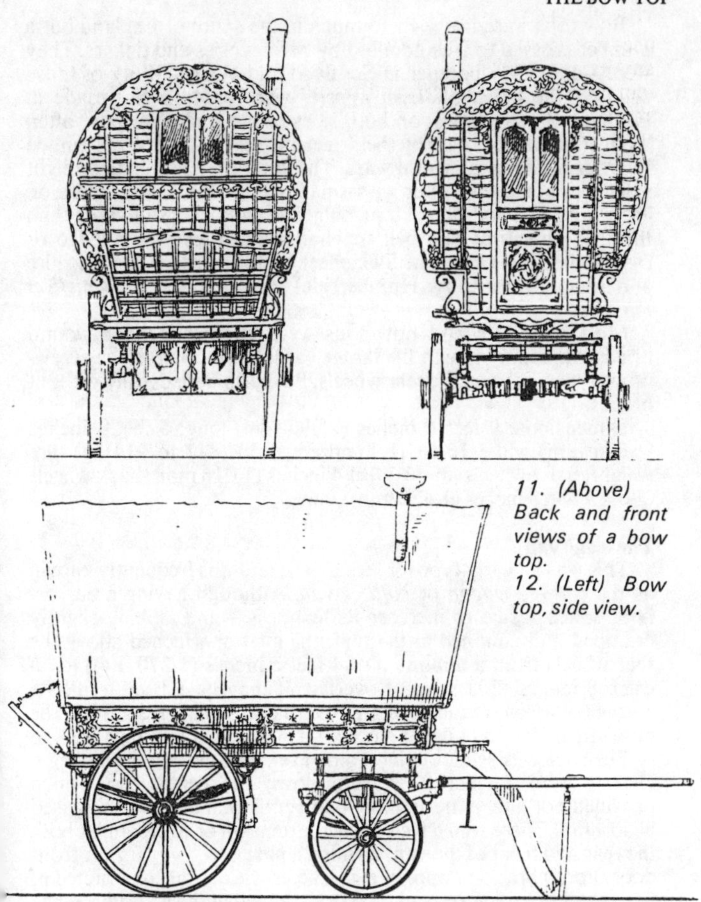

11. (Above) Back and front views of a bow top.
12. (Left) Bow top, side view.

front (half) door but no side windows, except on some square types.

Inner boarding of side planks or matchwood rose to waist height, above or beyond which was a patterned covering similar to a chenille tablecloth or light carpeting. Porches were lined with matchboarding, front and rear. As with the later open lot, the crownboard above the doorway was elaborately carved, while there was often rich carving between the ribs, in addition to chamfering.

The bow top being a light vehicle, the felloes of the wheels were narrow and elegant. Doors opened outwards.

Bow tops were not seen so much in the south of England but a number crossed to Ireland, used by both gypsies and tinkers. They were also widely popular in Scotland and Wales. Many of those used by the better-off Irish gypsies were ordered and made in England. Square bows, on both sides of the Irish Sea, were often 'bodged' or knocked up by their owners, although a few were made to order between the world wars. The latter may have had straight sides like bread vans, but with small windows near the centre on each side. Bell and barrel tops bulged even further outwards than the true bow top. The bell top had a fairly extensive ledge or overhang. Those made at Swinefleet on the borders of Yorkshire and Lincolnshire (now Humberside) were known as *Swinefleet tops*.

Most open lots and bow tops were fitted with hand-wound brakes, in common with the larger vans, these being of the screw-down type acting on the rear wheels. Pot carts were usually without brakes.

Dimensions: 9 feet 6 inches (2,896 mm) long; 5 feet 4 inches (1,626 mm) wide; 16 to 18 hundredweight (813 to 914 kg) tare weight; front wheels about 3 feet 4 inches (1,016 mm); back wheels about 4 feet 8 inches (1,422 mm).

The ledge van

This was an early type for larger vans and was frequently known as the *cottage wagon* or *cottage van*. Although having a narrow floor space – said to increase its lightness – and looking slightly cramped and confined at the rear, the interior widened above the rear wheels from a minimum of 4 feet 2 inches (1,270 mm) to an extra 8 inches (203 mm) of overlap. It may have been termed a cottage van on account of the overhang, which resembled the outward extension of upper storeys on many Tudor cottages.

The roof was semicircular, some examples eventually having a clerestory or mollicroft skylight down the centre top, which provided not only extra lighting and ventilation but also increased headroom. There was a well defined extension or overhang at both the rear and front of the van, forming a neat porchway for the front door. Porch brackets were of a characteristic design constructed of fine matchboarding or penny boards, shaped at the ends like wings or feathers, known as *feathering*. These were strengthened by T-shaped or Y-shaped iron brackets on either side. Some porch brackets were a continuation of the side boards of the bodywork, while others were fitted separately.

Side walls were ribbed with planks of matchboarding, fixed to carved and chamfered uprights or standards. Side walls below the ledges, however, were sometimes panelled with deeper planks and embellished with highly polished wood such as mahogany. The ledges were supported on the outsides by means of S-shaped scrolls in twisted brasswork – also known as brackets – but sometimes by

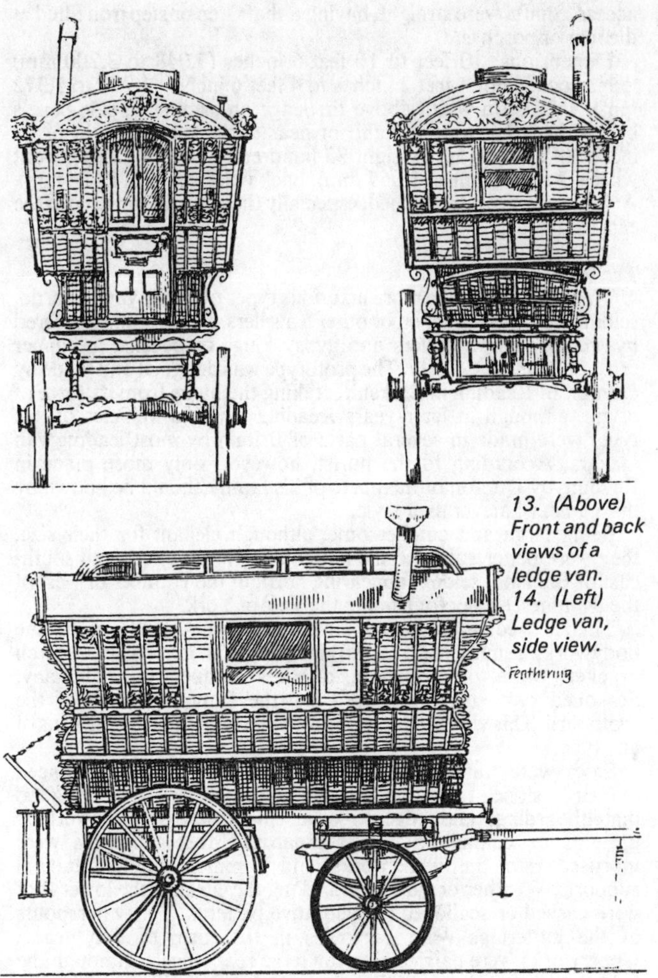

13. (Above) Front and back views of a ledge van.
14. (Left) Ledge van, side view.

uprights, both having barley-sugar curves.

An outside spindle rack or cage at the front porch end could be used for keeping fowls or as a storage place for small items.

Doorways were slightly to one side, off centre towards the right, allowing extra room on the narrow floor for the stove.

Steps, letting down to ground level, were carried at the rear of the van but hooked to the front, between the shafts, when needed for access. Shafts were straight, having a shaft step or step iron fitted at the rear or porch end.

Dimensions: 10 feet to 10 feet 6 inches (3,048 to 3,200 mm) long; floor width 4 feet 2 inches to 4 feet 6 inches (1,270 to 1,372 mm), with extra width above the ledge on each side; side panels below the ledge were upright, or near upright, to a height of 18 inches (457 mm); tare weight 28 hundredweight (1,422 kg); front wheels 3 feet 6 inches (1,067 mm); back wheels 5 feet (1,524 mm). Axle cases were lathe-turned, especially those made and used in the east Midlands.

The Reading van

This was among the more luxurious types of gypsy van or vardo, seldom used by showmen or other travellers. It was mainly ordered by wealthy horse dealers and gypsy kings or queens, the upper crust of Romany society. The prototype was designed and made by Dunton of Reading in Berkshire, taking the name from its town of origin, although in later years Reading vans (or vehicles of this type) were made in several parts of Britain by most leading van makers. According to the purist, however, only those made in Reading by Dunton or members of his family should be known by this name, whatever their style.

Being large and cumbersome, although elegant for their size, they were better suited to the flat country in the south and south-east of England, seldom appearing north of the Humber or west of the Pennines, except for a few in the Vale of York.

Timber used would be oak for the underworks and pine for the bodywork, usually with as straight a grain as possible. Porch brackets were of sycamore or (less frequently) mahogany. Seasoned oak was often used for the front or fascia of the footboard. This was similar for most of the larger and better vans of any type.

Sides were fairly straight but sometimes had a pronounced outward slope towards the roof. Bodywork was of good matchboarding, laid edge to edge, supported by near-vertical uprights or chamfered ribs (standards). Most standards were mortised into the underworks and summers or longitudinal supports. Weather or side boards along the edges of the lower roof were carved or scalloped in decorative patterns. The waterspouts of the gutterings were gargoyles in the form of lion heads. Upperworks were carried between large rear wheels, although the forewheels (as with most other types of van) were able to turn under the front platform in full lock.

Early types had a plain or arched roof but later vans were all fitted with a mollicroft or clerestory section. The mollicroft (which may have been named after its designer) was added after 1900 or 1901, although very few were seen before the summer of 1902. Most clerestories were about 10 inches (254 mm) high, curving

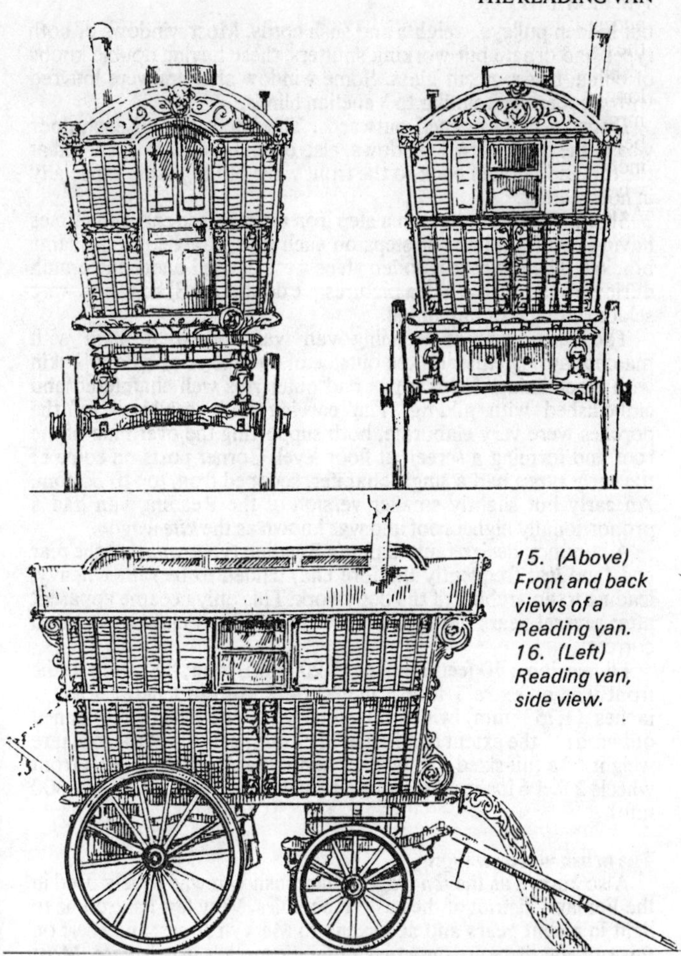

15. (Above) Front and back views of a Reading van.
16. (Left) Reading van, side view.

downwards at the front and rear towards the porches, but seldom reaching either end of the van roof. Some had square or flat ends, especially on the few Reading-type vans made by Wright of Leeds.

There were windows on both sides and at the rear end, each divided into several panes, with side shutters. Early types were casements or outward opening in the form of oblong wooden frames with single glass panes or panels. Later windows, introduced during the mid 1890s, were of the sash type, using inner but hidden pulleys, weights and sash cords. Most windows of both types had ornate but working shutters, these having double knobs of china, brass or cut glass. Some window shutters were louvred with wooden slats similar to Venetian blinds.

Doors usually opened outwards. The upper half of each door was in the form of two windows, also opening outwards, curved at the top and hooked back to the front walls of the porch, especially in hot weather.

Shafts were straight with a step iron at the porch end, sometimes having two footplates or steps on each side, attached to the same bracket. The main or wooden steps were carried under the cratch during transit. These had a picturesque double (or S) bend and were seldom straight or unpainted.

The early type of Reading van was somewhat plain with matchboarding either on the outside of the ribs or as a double skin with inner lining. Later types had outer ribs well chamfered and embellished with gilding. The carving and scrollwork of the porches were very elaborate, both supporting the overhang of the roof and forming a screen at floor level. Corner posts on some of the early types had a single chamfer, scooped from top to bottom. An early but slightly smaller version of the Reading van had a proportionally higher roof and was known as the *kite wagon*.

A common design fault of many Reading types was that the rear end (and less frequently the fore end) tended to be rather heavy, leading to an arching of the bodywork. This only became apparent after several years of roadwork but was difficult and expensive to correct.

Dimensions: 10 feet 6 inches (3,200 mm) long; the porch at the front was an extra 1 foot 5 inches (432 mm) in length; 5 feet 9 inches (1,753 mm) wide; on some vans the side walls leaned outwards to the extent of 4 inches (102 mm) per side at the top; tare weight of a full-sized van was 30 hundredweight (1,524 kg); front wheels 2 feet 6 inches (762 mm); back wheels 5 feet 3 inches (1,600 mm).

The brush van or wagon

Also known as the *fen wagon*, the brush van was widely used in the Fenland district of the eastern counties. Very few have come to light in recent years and according to Mervyn Jones, an expert on this subject, there are only two authentic models in existence. Most of them vanished from the roads well before the Second World War.

Although some may have been used by gypsies, they were mainly the property of other travellers, especially those making brushes, brooms and baskets for sale. There were racks and glass-panelled showcases along the sides, some protected by spindles, to display the stock of the owner, also a roof rack with iron side rails and a nameboard. During the 1920s motorised versions were

17. Brush wagon.

introduced, some converted from old army lorries of the First World War. These may have been responsible for the decline and disappearance of horse-drawn types, although the trade almost died out as a rural industry during the 1940s.

Another important feature of the brush wagon, both horse-drawn and motorised types, was the rearward facing door and porch, very rare among living vans, although a few of the larger vans ordered by showmen (especially the saloon type) may have had rear doors. Most other vans were approached and entered from the front or side, usually the former. Steps on the brush wagon were not removable, as they did not interfere with shafts or drawbar, and were kept in a fixed position. Most had handrails on either side of the steps, reaching to the doorposts.

The sides of the bodywork were either panelled or matchboarded but always straight or upright. Of heavy overall structure, the van appeared lighter than it was, being in plain colours without unnecessary carving or decoration. The underworks and materials used in construction were almost identical with those of the Reading type and other large vans.

The roof was a plain but shallow arch, without a mollicroft section, and frequently used for storage space. Brooms and brushes were usually carried at the sides and baskets on top.

Slightly longer and heavier than the Reading van, the brush wagon weighed up to about 40 hundredweight (2,032 kg) tare.

The Burton van

Also known as the showman's van and frequently used by the staff and proprietors of travelling funfairs and circuses, the Burton van was seldom used by gypsies as the small travelling wheels, fitting under the vehicle rather than at the sides, were better suited to main roads and streets than to rutted side lanes and the open heath. Gypsies also not infrequently drove their vehicles through shallow rivers and water splashes that needed a high clearance. In later years Burton vans were mainly hauled by steam traction engines or heavy lorries as part of a showman's road train. They were first made by Orton and Spooner at Burton upon Trent, Staffordshire.

Bodywork was not unlike that of the Reading van but less ornate, with straighter sides less inclined to lean outwards. The floor surface overhung the wheels at both back and front, for maximum interior living space. The arch of the roof was much shallower than that of the Reading and ledge types, usually having a deeper mollicroft roof or clerestory, similar to those on Pullman cars of the Midland Railway Company (the Pullman roof). Some vans had large flat panels of polished wood at the sides in place of matchboarding. Most axle cases were square and solid-looking, rather than turned or highly ornate. Many of the underparts for Burton vans and other showmen's wagons were made by the firm of F. J. Thomas of Chertsey, Surrey, and known as *Chertsey unders* or *Chertseys*.

There were often two windows on each side and one at the back. One side, however, was sometimes blind, as the smaller showmen used this as a backing for their stall or sideshow, also for advertising when on the road.

The door of a Burton van opened inwards, although the glass upper panels might open outwards.

When a van was parked, the front and rear ends were often supported by screw jacks, known as stanchion jacks, which eased the weight of the body above the wheels. Stanchion jacks were carried on most living vans owned by showmen.

Many Burton vans were fitted with a canopy or sun blind, as an awning of the front porch, mounted on corner props.

Luxury vans for showmen

These were the special types used only by the wealthier and more progressive showmen, from the late 1890s, but in later years drawn by a lorry or tractor unit and mounted on pneumatic tyres. There was no standard type or fixed dimensions and most were made to the whims of the people ordering them. They were not usually constructed by the traditional van and wagon makers but by those firms specialising in mobile fairground equipment of the heavier type, such as Savages of King's Lynn. An illustrated catalogue published by Savages in 1902 shows a large showman's living van

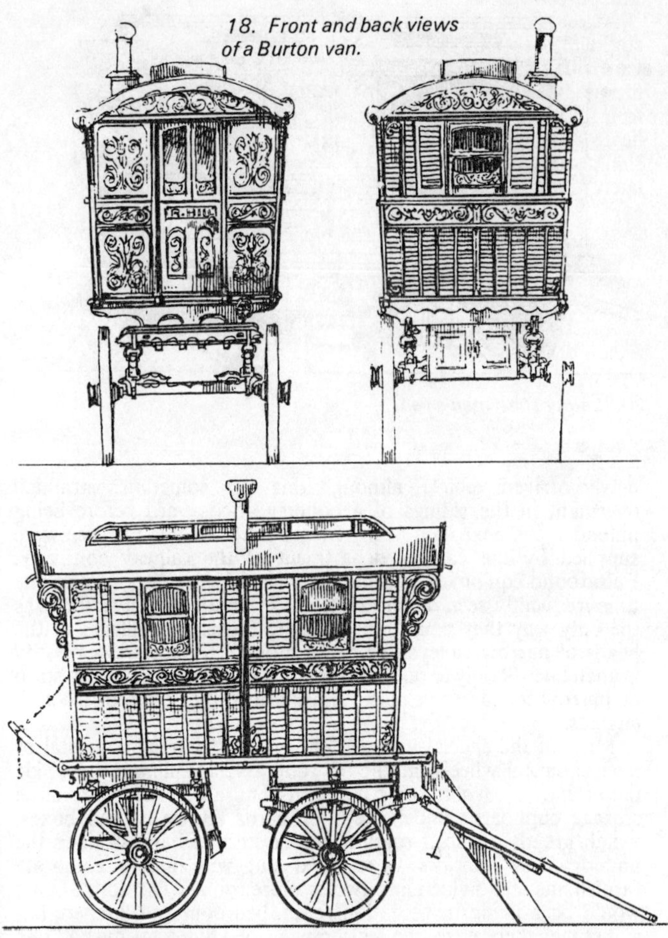

18. Front and back views of a Burton van.

19. Burton van, side view.

of the so called *saloon type*, with fully panelled sides, drawn by a single carthorse. As a rule, however, these needed a pair of horses or a larger team for even a short distance. Many were drawn to and from the showground by horses and run on to the flat trucks of the railway company, usually from an end-loading bay at the nearest station, continuing the journey by goods train. Teams of horses were hired at the other end of the line or sent in advance to meet the

20. Larger showman's van.

newly arrived vehicle, although this was sometimes stranded overnight in the sidings of a country goods yard before being unloaded the next day. Many horses used for this purpose were supplied by the cartage department of the railway company. Fairground equipment and the caravans of showmen were at one time frequently seen on special trains in South Wales, as this was the only way they could reach mining towns and villages at the heads of narrow valleys, for, while most of these were served by branch lines (if only to take out the coal), roads were often too steep or narrow for larger vehicles, either drawn by horses or traction engines.

Most of the special vans for showmen had small equirotal or near-equirotal wheels, mollicroft roofs of the Pullman type, side doors and removable steps but with handrails. There were large storage cupboards under the floorboards known as bellyboxes, which greatly reduced road clearance and perhaps strained the underframes. Interiors were fitted out with highly elaborate furnishings and divided into two or more rooms. The normal plan would be a living or reception room, bedroom and kitchen, but sometimes there were two bedrooms or two living rooms and one bedroom.

Early types had iron tyres while after the First World War lorry wheels from surplus War Department vehicles were used, these having deep, solid rubber tyres but thick wooden spokes. Pneumatic tyres came during the late 1920s and early 1930s.

Missionary vans

These varied almost as much as the special vans for well-to-do showmen, both in style and in dimensions. Some were straight-sided while others were of the ledge type, with overhang above the rear wheels. Many had a long wheelbase and resembled a type of pantechnicon or horse-drawn furniture van of the same period. Wheels were usually much smaller at the front than the back, the forewheels turning in full lock. Materials were even stronger and more substantial than those used in the construction of gypsy vans and the wagons of showmen. While the sides were straight and high, with plenty of headroom for the interiors, the arch of the roof might have been fairly shallow. The clerestory was usually of the end-to-end Pullman type, having slatted vents rather than glass lights. Side windows had shutters letting down from above rather than fixed at the sides. Many side windows were either round-topped or pointed (lancet) in an ecclesiastical design, reminiscent of church or chapel architecture. The front porch of the van was often protected by an arched or canopy roof of its own, used with a raised frontboard or dashboard as an improvised pulpit, from which crowds could be addressed at mass rallies. The stove pipe chimney frequently had a large revolving cowl, with an arrow-shaped weather vane showing the direction of the wind and helping the cowl to turn. Steps, almost like plain ladders, were propped against the side of the porch, at right angles to the main lines of the vehicle. The sides of the van were decorated with texts but they were

21. Missionary van, 1899.

sometimes hung with charts, religious pictures and symbols or enlarged hymn sheets.

Contractors' or corporation living vans

These were strictly utilitarian vehicles often with well floors but with shallow roofs. Some roofs were of corrugated iron, with a clerestory or ventilator in the centre top, having slats rather than lights. The flat sides of the van were made of heavyweight upright planks on a sturdy inner framework (the majority of living vans had horizontal planking or matchboarding). The exterior corner posts of the bodywork would have a single chamfer scooped from top to bottom.

There would be one or two small windows, one usually at the rear, with sashes and hinged or sliding shutters that could be padlocked. Tools were kept in a large chest or container, either under the bodywork in the form of a bellybox, or on a ledge at the rear of the living compartment. Wheels were usually of the heavy duty or wagon type but sometimes had iron or steel spokes and rims. Rear braking was operated by a screw-down wheel at the front of the van.

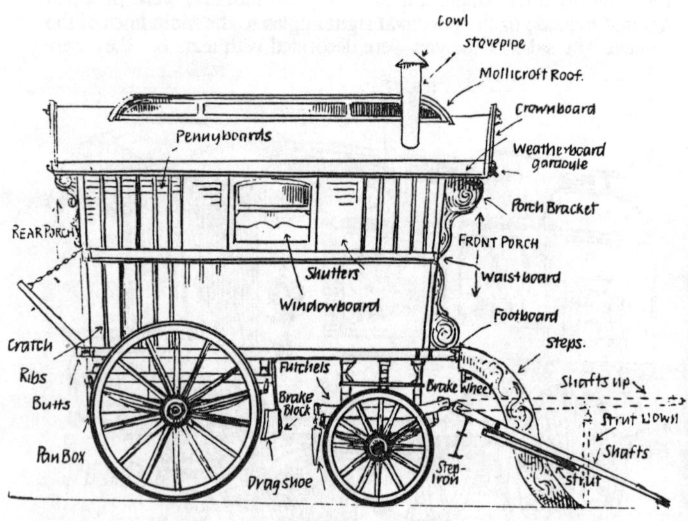

22. *Parts of a horse-drawn caravan.*

4. Construction of exteriors

The most important part of a caravan, and indeed of most types of horse-drawn vehicle, was the underworks or undercarriage. This would be made from the best well seasoned wood available, kept long enough in store (usually at the builder's yard) for what was known as a second shrinkage, before the final sawing up or dividing into parts. Clean straight timber was preferred, free from knots and notches.

All undercarriages were divided into forecarriage and hindcarriage, also known as lock (forelock) and cradle respectively. The forecarriage turned in full lock under the body of the vehicle and comprised an ash-wood framework of mainly cross members to which shafts or drawbar could be attached. Cross members at the fore end were attached under the bodywork by means of a kingpin or through pin, which acted as a pivot for turning the wheels. For extra stability in turning, two horizontal, highly greased wheel plates were used, in the form of a turntable. These were also known as ringplates and were about 3 feet 6 inches (1,067 mm) in diameter.

The longitudinal members forming the main framework of the forecarriage were known as *futchels* or *futchells*. There were up to six of them, held in place by grooved and notched cross pieces at right angles to the main lines of construction. Some of the futchels were curved in the form of a swan's neck or had a wavy appearance of repeated curves, mainly to improve their looks, although this was a matter of taste and not universal. Most futchels were projected well forward under the foot or front board, held in place by a splinterbar or rearward attachment for draught gear (shafts and so on). Splinterbars were lap-jointed on to the front upper parts of the futchels or mortised into the fore ends. Lap joints were always well bolted together and the top-mounted splinterbar was further reinforced by iron stays.

Semi-elliptical leaf springs were fairly long but shallow, as this was said to improve riding qualities, attached under both fore and rear carriages by means of loops or scrole irons, the latter being of several different patterns. Most leaves were of 5/16 inch (8 mm) steel plate, between seven and twelve in number, jack-bolted at the front and shackled at the rear. Patterns of scrole irons are explained and compared in figure 23, page 34. Springs were bolted through the centres of special hardwood blocks to the framework of the axle cases, further held in place by staple bolts and bolt plates. There were usually both side springs and inverted cross springs on each carriage.

A spreader or extension (draught) bar could be fitted to the right or offside part of the forecarriage, to which a second horse might be harnessed, either for extra draught on steep hills or for training

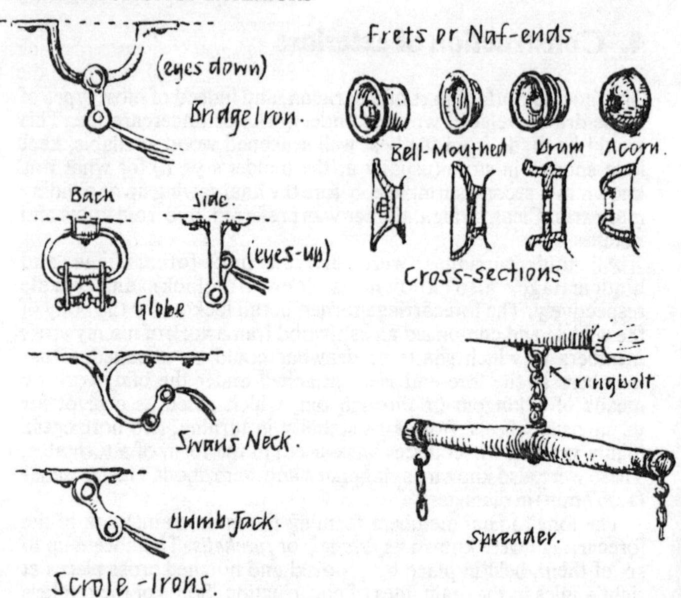
Frets or Naf-ends
(eyes down)
Bridgelron.
Bell-Mouthed
Drum
Acorn.
Back
Side.
(eyes-up)
Globe
Cross-sections
ringbolt
Swan's Neck.
Dumb-Jack.
Spreader.
Scrole-Irons.

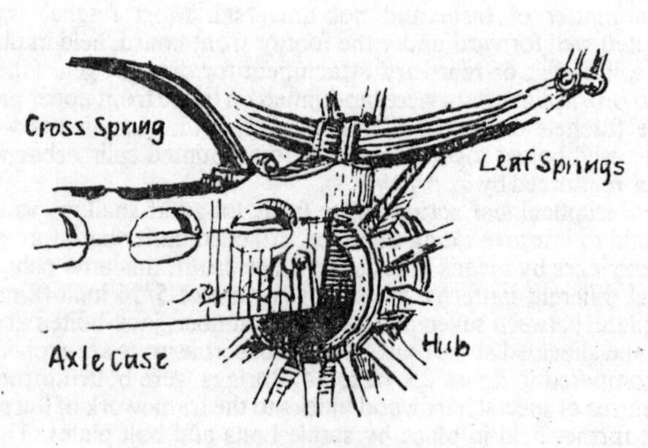
Cross Spring
Leaf Springs
Axle case
Hub
Detail of Suspension

Fig. 23.

purposes – breaking a young horse to traffic and roadwork. Such an item could be attached to a futchel or summer by means of a ring bolt. The extra horse was always in side draught, parallel with the shaft horse, and known for this reason as a *sider*.

The hind or rear carriage had two large crosswise members bolted directly to the summers or longitudinal members beneath the bed or bodywork of the van. These were 4 feet (1,219 mm) apart on most caravans. Scrole irons for the rearward springs were attached to longitudinal members, well chamfered, under the cross members (either one or two on each side) at least 2 inches (51 mm) from the sides of the van body. Projections or *butt ends* of all members were frequently carved with grotesque faces but sometimes merely chamfered.

Springs and scrole irons

Larger and heavier vans of the more elaborate type, particularly the Burton, brush and Reading types, would have a greater number of leaves. These all had *globe attachments* for their scroles with shackles fitted in the 'eyes up' position (see illustration). Smaller vehicles such as the bow top and ledge type had hanging or swan's neck bridge scroles, with shackles in the 'eyes down' position.

Wheels

It was generally considered that larger wheels were more elegant and stylish than those of smaller diameter, and also better in the long term for haulage over uneven surfaces.

Most wheels on horse-drawn caravans were slightly *dished*, the spokes forming a cone when each wheel was laid on its side. When turning in the upright position, directly under its load, the lowest spoke was always at right angles to the road surface, for extra strength and support where most needed; this was known as the *plumb spoke*. Most spokes were made of well seasoned wood, usually oak, while the outer sections of the rim, known as *felloes* (pronounced *fellies*, as they were originally spelt), were of ash. Each felloe or segment was made to hold two spokes. The number of spokes was variable but should always have been an even number, although some of the chariots and primitive wagons of antiquity were known to have had odd numbers. Many wheels had the spokes strutted for extra strength and durability, so that each alternate spoke was at least ½ inch (13 mm) further back from its neighbour. Most British-made living vans had either twelve spokes at the front and fourteen at the back or ten at the front and twelve at the back. Some of the flat carts and two-wheeled pot carts had up to sixteen spokes. Extra spokes were sometimes preferred on the more elaborate vehicles of wealthy showmen, especially those with wheels of small diameter but intended to carry additional weight. Showmen also had a great liking for infilling between the spokes, known as a *sunburst effect*. Each spoke has at least seven parts: the tenon or tongue, entering the hub at the centre of the wheel; the square-shaped shoulder, next to the hub, forming an attachment for the tenon; the front or front side near the hub; the throat, changing the shape of the spoke from square to oval section; the back or rear side, near the hub, behind the front; the body or oval part, sometimes pear-shaped, forming two-thirds of the length of the spoke; and the point of the spoke, which enters and attaches to the felloes.

The tyres that protect and encircle the wheel were at first made of iron but later of steel, which lasted much longer and was less likely to flake or crack. These were shrunk on to the wooden rims of the combined felloes while they were red-hot. The outer rim of each metal tyre was rounded but made to project slightly along the edges, preventing the painted surfaces of the wheel from scraping the kerb. A few of the more modern vans and larger vehicles, such as the showman's special and some of the later open lots, were mounted on pneumatic tyres but these were considered less seemly and traditional than iron or steel tyres by most travellers.

Hubs or centres of the wheels to which the spokes were tenoned, also known as stocks or naves, were of firm elm wood with a fibrous twisted grain unlikely to split or crack under pressure. They were held together, or further bonded, by means of narrow metal hoops, shrunk into position like band tyres when heated. Decorative frets or *nafs* (naf-ends) were attached over the outward terminations of each hub. These were mainly of turned brass but eventually of chromium plating, which was perhaps less attractive but easier to keep clean and well-polished. There were four main types of naf-end: two versions of the bell mouth (deep and shallow), and the less common drum and acorn types, as illustrated. The maker's name was frequently stamped on brass hubcaps but in later years these were interchangeable.

Axles

These were usually of a common type known as the *drabble axle*, subdivided into the Yorkshire or northern drabble and the London or southern drabble. The original drabble was nearer to the present Yorkshire version, having a short axle arm or stub for each wheel, attached to a central and crosswise axle case. With the London drabble a connecting length of iron, square in section, joined both arms together at the centre, although it must not be confused with the continuous axle. The outward extremity of the arm, stub or spindle fitted inside a tube of the inner axlebox, sometimes known as the pipe box, tapered for greater precision and smoothness of fit. The spindle arm was of turned steel. On the Yorkshire drabble, wheels fitted on short individual axle stubs were held in place by a flat wedge-like linchpin and washer, although on the London type fixed by two counter-threaded nuts. Both types were further protected at the outer extremities by brass grease caps, which held in the lubricants and kept out dirt and dust.

Axle cases, to receive and support the axle arms, were crosswise members, either straight across or arched towards the centres, made from seasoned elm wood. Curved axls were usually seen on the larger vans such as Reading and Burton types. The open lot frequently had a smaller dray-type case, often of double members in parallel, known as the Thompson dray case. Most types were skilfully chamfered and painted, although some were turned.

Bodywork

The body or upperwork of each van was usually of matchboarding, fitted one board above another by means of tongue and groove, like the floor of a building but in vertical or diagonal rather than horizontal positions. A few, however, were fitted by means of overlap. Stronger but narrower boards were known as penny boards, while a cheaper but wider variety were penny

24. (Top left) Brake block. (Top right) Porch of bow top. (Bottom) Turned axle case.

farthings. With some vans penny farthings were used for the sides and penny boards for roofs. The uprights to which the cross boards were attached were known as standards or ribs.

Some vans, especially those of showmen, frequently had external panelling of either polished or painted wood.

Shafts

These were known in different parts of Britain as *thills, sharves, shaves, rods* or *sharps*. They were secured to the splinterbar at the front of the forecarriage by ring bolts, through which a drawbar was passed, held in place by split pins.

Most good shafts were of ash at least 2½ inches (64 mm) deep but tapered towards the fore ends or extremities. They could be either curved or straight but the majority, especially on larger vans, were straight, on the horizontal plane, although narrower at the forward end and widening at the rear or van end, in conformation with the shape of the average horse. Those with an upward curve were usually attached to a low splinterbar. Some of the more expensive types were reinforced at the rear or van end by curved timbers on the insides, strap bolted throughout or fitted with bracket irons. Others had iron stays fitted on the diagonal at the rearward end. Butterfly chamfers made the shafts lighter, while adding to the attraction of their outward appearance.

Propsticks under the shafts appeared on most vehicles but were used more frequently on two-wheeled carts such as the pot cart or flat cart than on wagons or four-wheeled vans. These were known to most travelling folk as struts or shaft struts. When the shafts were propped or raised in a horizontal position, the vehicle could be mounted from a step iron or flat iron plate secured to the van end of the shafts by a metal stem or shank. Horizontal shafts, when the van or cart was resting, could be used for hanging out clothes, harness or blankets to dry, also for beating mats. The steps would only fit into place between the shafts when these were aligned with the bodywork and undergear.

Roofing

This consisted of several sheets of painted and weather-proofed canvas or cloth above thin planks, held in place by a framework of weatherboards round the sides, with arched crownboards at the centre front. The overhang of the porch at back and front (or front only) of a van would be supported by scrolls of carved wood known as porch brackets, some of which also fitted on to the base or floor of the porch, directly under the upper brackets. The roof was penetrated by a stovepipe chimney on the offside (plain-topped or cowled) and often by a vent for an oil lamp on the near side, both towards the front end of the van.

Large carriage or coach lamps were mounted under the front porch or at the front end of the van, while the brake wheel was

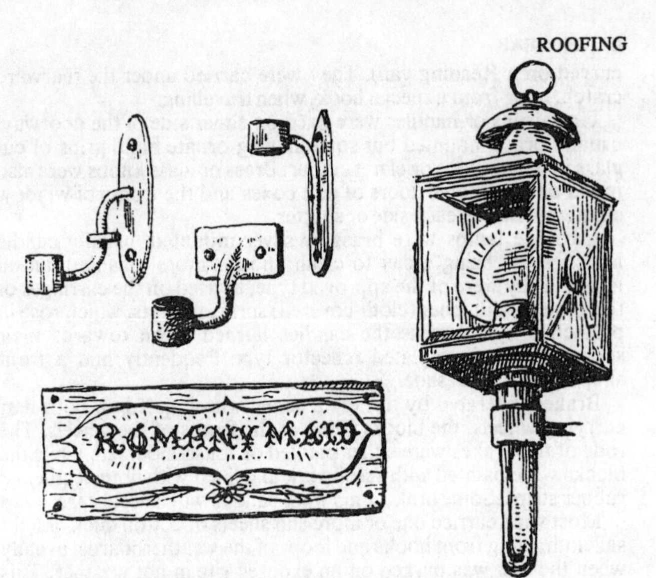

25. (Top left) Lamp irons. (Right) Porch lamp. (Bottom left) Nameplate over doorway.

usually on the nearside of the narrow footboard – looking forward – also under the overhang of the porch roof.

Outer gear

Most vans, especially the larger types, had a rearward shelf or cratch, in the form of an open framework. Protected by a canvas cover, this was a crude form of luggage rack, secured on either side by letting-down chains. There was also a pan box between the rear wheels, sometimes with an inner shelf, which could double as a hen coop or home for pet rabbits. Some vans also carried a side cage or coop (the spindle cage) for bantams and game fowl, from which the birds would be released on reaching a camp site, to peck about for themselves. If fowls were kept in the pan box this would have vents and the bottom of the box would be lined with hay or straw.

Some vans had a roller scotch (also known as a scotch roller) secured by chains to the hub of the nearside wheel at the rear. This prevented the van from rolling backwards on a slope, especially if the horse slipped before the application of the hand brake.

The drag shoe or skidpan, known in some country areas as the drugbat, was a hollow wedge fitted under the nearside rear wheel when a van was going downhill. When not in use this was hung in chains on the near underside of the vehicle.

Wooden steps, which fitted between the shafts when the caravan was resting or parked, were either straight or curved (usually curved on a Reading van). They were carried under the rearward cratch, hung from a special hook, when travelling.

Grab irons or handles were fixed on either side of the doorway, usually brass-mounted but some having ornate hand grips of cut glass in a dark wine or claret colour. Brass or glass knobs were also found on the double doors of pan boxes and the fronts of window shutters – two on each side or shutter.

Carriage lamps were brass or silver mounted, usually candle lamps, these being easier to clean and far more reliable than oil lamps. They were of the approved type, as used on the carriages of the gentry, with inner (cloth-covered) spring mounts, which rose in protective cylinders as the candles burned down towards their sockets. The silver-plated reflector type frequently had a front shaped like a horseshoe.

Brakes, operated by turning a screw-wheel, acted on both rear carrying wheels, the blocks being at the fronts of the wheels. The rods of the brakes were either painted or brass-mounted, while the blocks were painted with scrollwork and lined with fibre, leather or rubber strips. Some brake arms were banded with sheet brass.

Most vans carried one or more sun sheets of cotton duck or light sailcloth, hung from hooks and loops of the weatherboards, usually when the van was parked on an exposed site in hot weather. This protected the paintwork and varnish from blistering, kept the van cool inside and provided an extra side tent or room against a wall of the vehicle. These sheets were not proofed and were sometimes used, on a semi-permanent site, to preserve the van from interior condensation and general exposure.

Other items carried included buckets, baskets, a light ladder used for mending the roof and chimney, and a hooked pole to disentangle the roof and stovepipe from overhanging branches or to cut down dead wood for firewood.

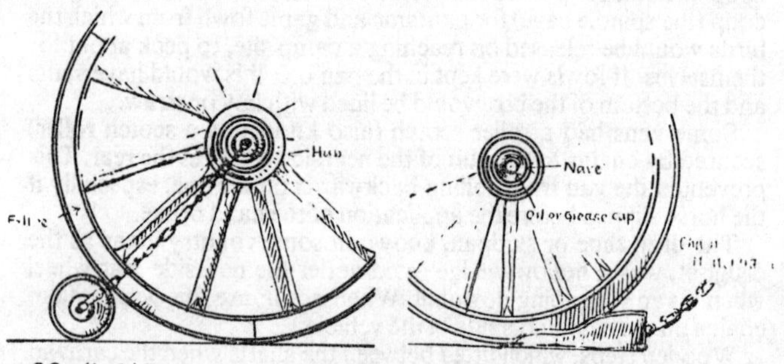

26. (Left) Roller scotch. (Right) Dragshoe.

5. Interiors

Considering its small size, it is amazing how much could be fitted into the living quarters of the traditional horse-drawn caravan, which often seemed far more roomy than all but the most luxurious trailer. The height above ground level added to this feeling of spaciousness, which may have been an optical illusion but provided a feeling of comfort and security lacking in vehicles nearer the ground.

Much of the furniture and many fittings of the horse-drawn van were built in rather than freestanding, made of good quality deal, often veneered, but sometimes of solid mahogany. Wherever possible it tended to be bowed or rounded at the front rather than square, both for greater safety and to conserve space. The larger or special vans ordered by wealthy showmen, however, had much of their furnishings freestanding and are worthy of separate consideration.

Both gypsies and showmen tended to be conservative and traditional, perhaps less dominated by whims of fashion than people with fixed abodes. In matters of interior furnishing there was also a strong sense of fitness for purpose. Utilitarian requirements often coincided with aesthetic aspects so that vans furnished for the greatest comfort and convenience were usually those appearing in the best taste with traditional layout and fittings. Ultra-modern furnishings in such a setting would be unthinkable, although in later years, especially in smaller vans, such monstrosities as the simpering child and grinning Alsatian dog (in glazed china or painted plaster of Paris) were not unknown, along with gimmicky fire irons and hearth tidies, fake horse brasses being almost as popular in some open lots as in a modern suburban home.

With the brush van, which had the door and entrance steps at the rear, most furnishings were in reverse, with a cross bed at the front rather than the back of the vehicle. Burton vans, with two windows on each side, frequently had the stove placed between them rather than on the left-hand side of the door, near the entrance.

With the open lot type of van the stove projected well into the centre of the van, rather than being tucked away in a niche or compartment. There were no locker seats in this type of van, the seating of the inner ledge increasing the feeling of spaciousness where it was most needed. Some ledges, however, were only a few inches wide and could not have been very comfortable for larger people.

With early vans of the larger type there were two end or bed posts from floor to ceiling, to which doors could be hinged, enclosing the lower berth at will. These doors were later replaced by slides and the uprights either removed or not included in the general structure when a new van was built. Some vans, however, had slides for the upper berth and hinged doors for the lower berth.

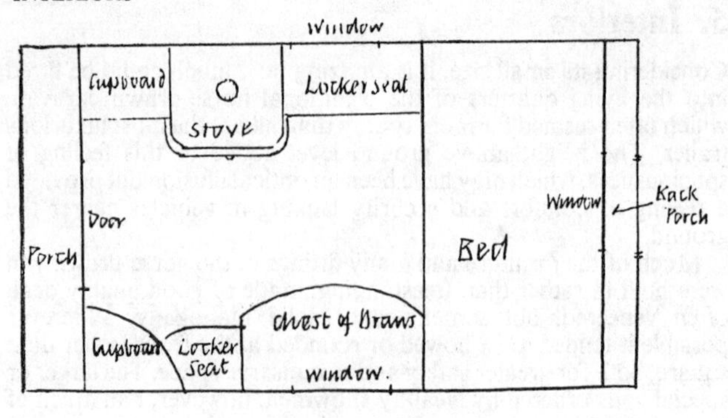

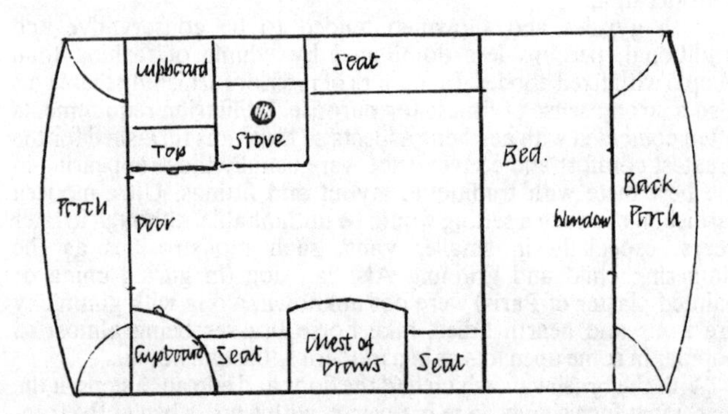

27. (Top) Interior plan of Reading van. (Bottom) Interior plan of bow top wagon.

A shelf or sill ran across the upper rear part of the upper berth, having a protective spindle rail of brass. Early bed places were curtained off but later types had slides or panels with mirrors on the exteriors. The side of the top berth, furthest from wall and window, had a protective side rail or board to prevent a person sleeping on the outside from rolling out of bed. In smaller vans, such as the bow top, beds pulled out on wooden side rails, increasing their size from single to double by manual adjustment. There were drawers and pull-out tables between upper and lower berths of open lot and bow top, while sliding tables also appeared in some Reading vans.

Locker seats at the sides of the van fitted into spaces beside and opposite the stoves, in larger types. Some of these had lifting tops or lids with shallow cupboards or drawers nearer floor level.

On the right of the entrance, seen from the front porch, was a bowed or bulged cupboard, having a glass-fronted door at the top and panelled drawers or cupboards below. Opposite the bowed cupboard might be a wardrobe, not found in smaller vans, which had to make do with drawers and clothes chests. Cutlery and some china were kept in drawers or shallow cupboards with a gilded and triangular (pedimented) top, above the seat opposite the stove. These drawers had cut glass or china knobs while other drawers had brass (tug) handles.

Bow tops and open lots frequently had china display cabinets recessed into the side of the van, opposite the stove, with nests of shallow drawers or cupboards above.

The Burton or showman's van would have a small iron safe in a further recess, away from the door, bolted to the floor of the van. Gypsies tended to be more careless with their money, even when engaged in a steady line of business such as horse dealing or carpet selling. Some were once thought to have secret hiding places in their mattresses, under the floorboards or in panels of furniture, but most of these ideas have been dismissed as the kind of tale travelling folk like to tell about themselves. Most gypsies, in particular, kept their money in belts, purses or money bags secreted on their persons.

Ceilings

The ceilings of the open lot and the bow top were lined with a form of covering or carpeting, at least in part. After the First World War, however, a sheet of painted or printed felt often replaced the traditional chenille or sometimes appeared in the middle of the roof with a narrower lining of chenille lower down on each side. Numerous designs were painted or stencilled on the centre parts, ranging from stars and planets to flowers, bunches of grapes and clusters of vine leaves. Most open lots had a thick layer of inner felt beneath the chenille.

The larger vans such as Reading, Burton and ledge types had boarded ceilings, under an outer roof of proofed canvas and lighter penny boards. The supporting beams or ribs often showed through, both as a structural feature and for decorative effect. These were chamfered, gilded, painted and lined out in a manner similar to the outer ribs of the main bodywork. The classical acanthus leaf and egg and dart motifs were frequently used for both interiors and exteriors. Some ceilings of the more expensive vans were boarded over as a double skin, a lining that continued down both side walls as a means of protective insulation. Inner roof boards were often painted in light colours but also grained and stained in light or dark oak, a feature shared with many stern cabins of canal boats.

Interior panels of the skylight, clerestory or mollicroft roof were frequently sky blue, sometimes lined out at the edges or decorated with scrollwork and gold leaf. There were often double brass rails fixed to the lower interior parts of the skylight.

Windows

Most windows had removable window or cross boards, fitting over the lower section for protection and greater privacy. These were carved and painted on the outside and painted, lined and sometimes gilded on the inside. They had carved or rounded tops and were about 9 or 10 inches deep (225–250 mm).

Window shutters sometimes had hinges but usually slid in shallow grooves.

Beds

The *bed place* was at the upper end of the van, in a crosswise position, opposite the door. There were usually two beds or berths, directly above each other, as though in the cabin of a ship or barge. Maximum dimensions of the upper berth, normally used by the parents or heads of the family, were 6 feet long by 3 feet 4 inches wide (1,829 by 1,016 mm), although a lower or child's berth (bunk) may have been slightly shorter or narrower, especially in caravans with outward sloping side walls. In ledge vans the under berth was a mere 4 feet 6 inches (1,372 mm) long, either very cramped or suitable only for a small child. Other members of the family slept outside the van in tents known as bender tents or *benders*, or in bed boxes on flat carts, similar to the pot cart. Some would even sleep under the van or cart, especially in summer. At one period only the youngest children and the senior members of the family slept in real beds inside the van. In fine weather most gypsy people of any age preferred to sleep under the stars, their light mattress stuffed with hay, straw, heather or horsehair.

Bedclothes and furnishings were the best the van dweller could afford, with fine linen pillow cases, good quality Witney blankets and quilted, tasselled eiderdown or counterpane. The mattress and bolster would be stuffed with down or under-feathers, above a straw mattress or palliasse covered with striped ticking. Bed curtains were of velvet or silk, far more luxurious than anything found in most cottages or farmhouses along the traveller's route.

Window coverings and floor coverings

Curtains were of silk (lustrine), satin or velvet, trimmed at the borders with lace, crochetwork or tufted bobbles. Bobbles were very popular from the late 1890s, also appearing along the tops of shelves, the edges of drawers, cupboards and overmantels or mantelpieces. Some windows had pull-down blinds in addition to ordinary curtains, these being on spring rollers, operated by pulling on a centre or side cord.

Floors had both linoleum and carpets, also mats and rugs, all of good quality. It was found advisable, however, to remove linoleum from time to time to prevent sweating and rotting of the floorboards. Some gypsies made and sold rugs or acted as agents for various types of floor coverings.

Bow tops and open lots frequently had storage places, used mainly for clothes, behind an arras or upright screen of curtains, suspended from brass wires.

Most van dwellers kept their mobile homes in immaculate condition, taking up the rugs and carpets at regular intervals and beating them while laid across the propped-up shafts.

Stoves

These could be used for both cooking and heating but mainly the latter. Many gypsies, also a number of showmen and other travellers, preferred to cook at least some of their meals on an open fire, burning dry wood, collected locally, on what was known as the *yog*. The indoor stove was used mainly in cold and wet weather or for brewing strong tea, a drink to which most British van dwellers were greatly addicted.

Early vans may have had open grates or hearths, but these were considered both unsafe and dirty. They were later replaced, except in the larger vans of showmen, by an enclosed stove or stove with side oven. This was kept in a recess, near the door, the sides of which were lined with upright plates of enamelled iron decorated with fluted patterns or arabesques. Above the recess would be an overmantel and shelf, protected by front rails and bedecked with bobbles, on which might be displayed Staffordshire figures and flat or half-back ornaments of china and brass.

There were eventually three or four types of stove used in living vans, some of which are still made and in daily use. These were mainly coal burners rather than coke or oil stoves. The first and perhaps the most important of these was the *Colchester* or brass-fronted wagon stove, often known as 'the policeman in the corner', being tall, massive and upright. This dated from the eighteenth century in style and tradition, descended from the prototype designed by Count Rumford for cottagers and travellers, although produced for the retail market at a factory in the Essex town of Colchester, controlled by the firm of Beard and Son, since the 1780s. The front of the stove was of solid brass kept polished like a looking glass.

A later but perhaps smaller and more convenient stove known as the *Hostess* was introduced during the 1890s, made by the firm of Smith and Wellstood. This could be ordered direct from the makers but was usually supplied through general stores and ironmongers in market towns.

The latest development was a small but fanciful stove known as the *Queen stove* or *Queenie*, ideal for smaller vans or outdoor camping. It proved highly efficient and economical, certainly a space-saver as it was only 20 inches (508 mm) high and 15 inches

(381 mm) across. These were first made about the time of the First World War and are still used in some open lots, also being exported to the United States of America for camping and other purposes. They could be bought for as little as 10 shillings (50 pence).

Some van dwellers bought small marine stoves, as used on the larger yachts and coastal barges, or even in the galleys of small tramp steamers. These were appropriately known as *skipper stoves*.

Stovepipe chimneys were tall and straight, usually placed above the right or offside of the van, near the crown of the road and as far as possible from overhanging hedges or branches of trees. Accidents or entanglements, however, were not unknown, especially in narrow lanes.

Various copper, brass and iron utensils or implements were hung round the stove, in its recess. These included a lid lifter for both stove and pan lids, oval or round cooking pans and stewpots, a bucket-handled frying pan for the yog or outdoor cooking, various fire irons and a highly polished copper kettle, which would have a narrow, serrated spout and a large ball or acorn shaped knob in the centre of the lid. Most kettles held a maximum of 8 pints (4.55 litres).

Lamps and lighting effects

There were both wax candles on side brackets and brass or chromium paraffin lamps in most vans.

The most elaborate of these oil lamps were provided by the firm of Mellor and Sons of the Owl Lamps Works, Oldham. These were also supported on side brackets and known by some as *angel lamps* from the figure like an angel engraved on the design. The lower part of the fount was of cut glass, shaded or stained a deep red, while the globe was often hand-painted. Most vans had oil lamps in pairs, on swivel brackets or bases.

Interiors of larger vans owned by showmen

Perhaps the largest and most elaborate of these vans, eventually hauled by a traction engine, was owned by William Murphy, the fairground showman and riding master (owner of steam roundabouts with gallopers or galloping horses). This cost about £4,000 before the First World War and was constructed by the Staffordshire firm of Orton and Spooner, makers of the famous Burton vans. It was well over 30 feet (9.1 m) long and weighed 10 tons. There was an elaborate grate and overmantel, this being mainly for show, as the van was fitted with electric lights, fires and even radiators, all well in advance of the times. Although perhaps over-elaborate (but not fussy) by modern standards, it was furnished in what was then the height of good taste and comfort, with deeply padded armchairs, bevelled looking glasses, delicate porcelain figures on the mantelpiece and mahogany panelling.

There were three separate rooms, most of the furniture, including beds, chairs and tables, being freestanding.

Some wealthy showmen became so attached to their vans that even when owning a modern villa or country house, to which they might retire during the winter season, they preferred to camp out in the garden or back yard, keeping the house merely as a status symbol or as a place where younger members of the family might entertain their friends. One retired traveller gave up his life of roving to buy a house but eventually demolished a side wall so that he could bring his caravan into the living room.

Missionary vans

The sleeping quarters in these vans, with bunks or cross beds, were curtained or partitioned off from the rest of the interior, although seldom a separate room. This type of van had a high standard of comfort but few decorations, apart from framed texts or prints of religious subjects. Chests, shelves and cupboards would be needed for books, tracts and the pamphlets distributed to would-be converts. There was usually a built-in wardrobe used for both ordinary clothes and vestments. The front of the van, under its canopy roof, might be used as a pulpit for open-air services and impromptu sermons. Rodney Smith or 'Parson Smith', the evangelist preacher and missionary of gypsy origins, often addressed seven thousand people or more at a time from the porch of his van.

George Borrow, in *Lavengro*, records how he spent some time during the 1820s or 1830s in the company of a Welsh missionary preacher and his wife. This elderly couple appeared to be touring the Welsh Marches in a type of pot cart but slept under the stars except in very cold or wet weather. Many of the later missionaries preferred a much higher standard of comfort and, although some vans had bunks, they often slept at inns or in houses to which they might be invited by lay members of their sect, also devoted to the cause. In the latter case their van was not so much a home as a mobile chapel and vestry.

The American gospel wagon had the interior fitted out with a number of benches on the longitudinal plan, with a central space for the choir and lay speakers or ministers. There was a side entrance and steps that could be let down, from the top of which an even larger congregation might be addressed. Most were semi-open but large enough to accommodate an organ or band of instrumental players. The first vehicle of this type was built by the wagon-building firm of Pearce and Lawton (Washington, DC) in 1887.

Contractor's or corporation vans

These had the bare minimum of interior furnishing, including a seat locker, stove and sleeping bunk, the latter lowered from a side wall on letting-down chains. Some vans of this type also had a form of desk locker, fixed to the end wall near the window, used for written work and keeping accounts. As with the showman's van, there would often be an iron safe in the corner. Half doors opened outwards and resembled those of a stable or barn. In their strict utility and lack of elegance they were the exact opposite of the showman's van or Romany vardo.

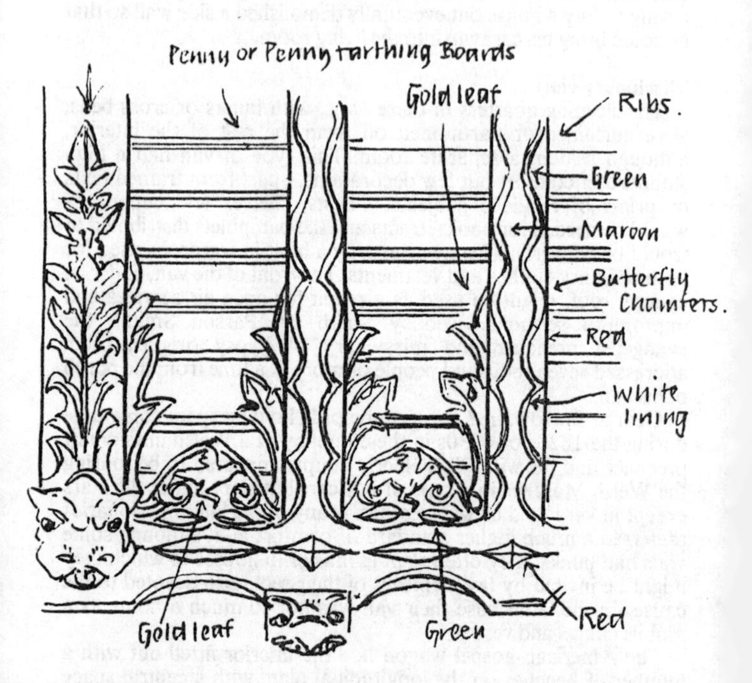

28. Chamfering and construction of bodywork on a Reading van.

6. Paintwork and decoration

The painting and decoration of living vans was seen at its best on vehicles made for gypsies. Even those vans used by showmen, apart from a few of the larger specials and saloon types, by comparison lacked flair or imagination in their decoration. Brush vans were usually plain and unadorned, as were the vans of missionaries, contractors and council or corporation workers. Those used in public works appeared in variations of several plain but drab and often hard-wearing colours, from battleship grey to camouflage green. Only the gypsy vans had a wealth of carving or full chamfering of almost every visible member.

Most vans were painted in the yard or workshop of the constructor but frequently under the direction or to the specifications of the new owners, who were sometimes allowed to camp in tents or other vans on the premises. Some of the smaller vans were painted or touched up by the gypsies or showmen themselves.

There was a bright but limited range of colours, partly dictated by tradition, especially among the gypsies, and partly because those selected were the easiest to mix and the most readily available. All van painters ground and mixed their own pigments rather than buying them ready made in cans or drums. This was both cheaper and more effective, especially during the Victorian era, when ready-mixed colours were of good quality but harder to find than their ingredients and most craftsmen, from house painters to boat and vehicle painters, preferred to grind and mix for themselves, labour costs being less important than in modern times. The main colours were maroon or dark red (similar to the red used by the London, Midland and Scottish Railway between the world wars), a lighter and brighter red with more orange in its composition – near vermilion, a medium green similar to Hooker's Number 2 in the artist's paintbox, and a strong yellow. These formed the basic groundwork of all colour schemes connected with van painting, apart from the exceptions mentioned earlier. Other colours such as lighter greens, purple, blue and violet were used for small details incidental to the main theme and rarely, if ever, for large areas of body or upperworks. White, pale yellow or grey for the bodywork were described by gypsies as 'poverty colours'.

Underparts of the van were a pale lemon yellow or salmon pink, but in many cases they were left unpainted, allowing the woodwork to breath, although this seems to have been a matter of personal choice. A dark yellow paint between umber and ochre was sometimes used in place of gold leaf when that was considered too expensive, but it was regarded as skimping and cheeseparing by most customers. White was used in various parts for details and lining out, especially on the ribs or standards and their complex chamferings, which was where the greatest amount of gold leaf also appeared. All woodwork was treated with flat non-gloss paint (gloss paint being a recent invention), given at least three layers of protective varnish.

The aim of external paintwork was to protect the van but also to emphasise and enhance its character, although amateur and non-gypsy owners (not directly connected with showmanship or entertainment) tended to play this down, especially when the mobile home was used for holidays and land cruising. Gypsies and many showmen, on the other hand, detested pastel or neutral colours and sought the cheerful ostentation more sophisticated or self-conscious owners tried to avoid.

Some of the best and most effective painting, especially scrollwork, small designs and pictorial motifs, was to be seen on the bow tops and open lots, which had larger, flatter surfaces, below the overhang, to decorate, not superimposed by ribs or standards. There were many interesting and often freehand designs spontaneously developed, from simple brush strokes and arabesques, many painted by the gypsies themselves. This was a true form of inspired folk art, closely akin to the roses and castles painted on the canal craft of owner boaters.

The horse and horseshoe motif appears on many living vans, especially those owned by gypsies, even on the motor-drawn trailers of modern travellers. Horses were not only creatures of great importance to Romany people but a symbol of good luck (especially the grey horse) and the means by which travelling folk moved from place to place. From times immemorial gypsies have traded in horses and ponies, using them for drawing vans and in earlier times as pack animals, while many of their race were wayside shoesmiths or harness makers and repairers, dependent on horses for their livelihood, pleasure and essential needs. It is not surprising, therefore, that horses and anything to do with them should feature so much in their design schemes. While heads of horses in small panels were the most numerous, rearing, standing, walking and trotting horses (especially on the double doors of rearward pan boxes) are the most interesting and spirited. These, with horseshoes and sometimes riding crops or driving whips, were to the van dweller what roses and castles had been to the canal boater.

Carving

Much hand carving was done for both utility and decorative effect, especially the chamfering of the uprights and chief members of the bodywork, which decreased overall weight without sacrificing strength. Most of this was done in the builder's yard but frequently by local men working on commission or contract and brought in for the purpose. Carving on doors, porch brackets and weatherboards, on the other hand, was purely decorative and may sometimes have been done by the gypsy owners in their spare time. Certain patterns of carving, especially porch brackets, are also associated with particular makers.

Carvings of human or animal heads were sometimes copies from larger works found in churches or on public monuments and other buildings, which might have been admired by a prospective van owner. Most builders kept samples and patterns as a guide but were open to any reasonable suggestions, frequently working from rough sketches made by the customer.

Popular motifs for carvings were bunches of grapes, vine leaves, flowers, small birds in flight, horses, human or animal heads (especially lions, some perhaps influenced by heraldic gateways to country mansions or by inn signs), with many fabulous beasts such as griffins and dragons. Waterspouts from the gutterings were often in the form of a traditional gargoyle or demonic grinning face, but more frequently the head of a lion, the projecting spout clenched between its front teeth. Vans constructed in the seaport towns of the north-east such as West Hartlepool would have an array of curious fishes, shells and sea monsters. The latter were frequently seen on Burton-type vans, many of which were eventually made in this area. It appears that many of the men working in these northern yards had frequently served at sea as ship's carpenters or worked in docks and shipyards, perhaps carving or painting the figureheads of ships in the Baltic trade.

Axle cases on most vans were richly carved and chamfered, reducing overall weight by at least an eighth part without reducing strength and reliability. This was highly skilled work performed with drawknife or spokeshave, using different lengths of scoop or cut to suit the particular area to be carved. Other axletrees or cases were either turned on a lathe or partly turned and partly hand-carved, combinations seen to their greatest advantage on ledge wagons and certain bow tops. Showmen, however, seemed to have a great dislike for turned axle cases. When finished and painted the scoops or chamfers were lined out, this being done freehand, using special lining brushes of large or small types known as *swords* and *daggers* respectively. Templates or stencils were sometimes used on the vehicles of showmen, but most gypsies preferred freehand and original work so that no two vans were exactly alike.

Patterns of chamfering were mainly butterfly (frequently used on shafts) of outward curving sections, or inward curving and known as scollops. Apart from the double-handed spokeshaves and drawknives, some carvers used a curved and pointed *peg knife* (also used for making clothes pegs and in basketwork), with a whole range of chisels and gouges, both straight and round or hollow.

7. Van builders

Those specialising in making vans for gypsies and other travellers were usually craftsmen living in towns or villages on their main routes or in localities renowned for markets, race meetings or annual fairs attended by such people. Others may have been situated near areas where there was seasonal work, such as hop picking, in which travelling folk were known to share. Such men left few papers or written records, through lack of either education or more conventional contacts – mainly dealing with people who were themselves unlettered – so that by now only a few of the more outstanding makers are remembered, a mere handful where there may have been large numbers.

Perhaps the most renowned of all the van builders was Dunton of Reading in Berkshire, the designer and first maker of the Reading van. Dunton and his sons were also noted for their ledge vans and other similar vehicles. They were renowned for high standards of workmanship and decoration, especially for their elegant futchels and curved van steps and for axle cases surmounted by blocks that bridged or covered the upper part of the axle arm near the inner hub. They made vans and carts for all types of owner but mainly for gypsies and only rarely for showmen. They had a yard on Highbridge Wharf from the 1870s, although established much earlier in a different part of the town, but only made living vans from the 1880s. Most of the painting and gilding was done by a nephew, George Dunton, who died shortly after the First World War. The business changed hands in 1922 and passed to Froud, Rivers and Kernutt, who merely repaired and refurbished older vehicles. During the First World War Alfred Dunton, son of the founder, worked on government contracts repairing army wagons. In later years he was urged to extend his work to making and repairing the bodies of motor vehicles with backing from the War Department but claimed there was 'no future in motor transport', missing the chance of a lifetime. His own son was so disheartened by this lack of enterprise that he gave up vehicle work and turned to shopfitting.

Another famous builder in the south of England was F. J. Thomas of Chertsey, Surrey, renowned not only for his own vans but for the supply of new undercarriages to showmen and other vehicle builders. These were the famous Chertsey unders, previously mentioned.

William Wheeler of Guildford, Surrey, also made numerous vehicles for showmen and travellers but turned to motor vehicles during the early days of the First World War.

In London D. Macintosh was the main builder of gypsy vans and carts, having a yard at Upper Norwood, an area then widely visited by many gypsies travelling south of the Thames, renowned both as a meeting place and as a venue for winter quarters, especially in the neighbourhood of Gypsy Hill. During the 1920s considerable building expansion took place in this area, having begun in a small way even before the war, restricting and finally destroying most of the camp sites, so that Macintosh was forced into premature retirement.

King of Wisbech and Leonard of Soham, both in Cambridgeshire, made high quality Burton-type vans but mainly on Chertsey unders, while Sykes and Godbolt in Norfolk made brush wagons for the brush and basket makers of the Fens. Godbolt had a well known yard at Norwich where many of his vans were assembled, distinguished by lifelike carvings in bas-relief of Saint George slaying the dragon.

Savages of King's Lynn were better known for their fairground equipment, traction engines and agricultural machinery but produced several large vans for well-to-do showmen until the 1900s. These were known as Pullman or saloon-type vans, with long low bodies, better suited for mechanical rather than animal traction. Known as 'horse killers' even in their own day, some were trundled as far as the nearest station and loaded on to flat trucks, while others may have been pulled by elephants belonging to the showmen, as were some of the Burton vans in the Bostock and Wombwell Menagerie of the 1900s.

In the west of England the largest builders of horse-drawn vehicles were the Bristol Waggon and Carriage Works Limited, which eventually produced everything on wheels from gypsy vans to lifeboat carriages and from hand barrows to motor cars. They were founded during the early 1850s by two Quaker brothers, a branch of the same family also making Fry's chocolate and cocoa. They failed, however, to survive the economic depression between the world wars and closed during the late 1920s. It was the Bristol Waggon and Carriage Works that constructed the *Wanderer* for Dr Stables, this being the first holiday or pleasure van ever made, now preserved in Bristol Industrial Museum.

Further west, at Bridgwater, Somerset, the firm of Watts and Company was renowned for its Burton-type vans, many with panelled mahogany sides rather than matchboarding. In Hereford there were two notable builders constructing vans for gypsies in the Welsh Marches, at one time a popular area for travellers on account of the seasonal fruit and hop picking. These were H. Jones and Son and George Cox and Company. Although there were no lasting contacts between them, Cox had served Jones as an apprentice and traded under the name of 'Cox and Co, late Jones and Son', adding to the confusion. Both firms constructed ledge and Burton vans, Cox claiming to have built the last authentic all-timber van (ledge type) for a branch of the Smith family in 1938. He constructed several bow tops and open lots up to 1945 and later turned to the restoration of old vans and scale modelling. One of his professional carvers was of German origins, producing highly skilled work but with an unmistakable continental touch, redolent of the Black Forest rather than the Black Mountains.

Many fine vans were produced in the Midlands, especially at or near Burton upon Trent, where the Burton van for showmen was first designed and constructed. One of the outstanding firms from this part of Staffordshire was Orton and Spooner, both partners being engineers and wagon builders, having served their apprenticeships at Savages of King's Lynn. For over forty years this firm was renowned for Burton vans, many with superior external decorations. There were several makers in Derbyshire, including W. Watson and later a Herbert Varney of Belper. Varney and Company produced many bow tops and general work for fairgrounds, circuses and menageries but closed in 1926.

In the north of England the seaport town of West Hartlepool was an important centre for van making, being the winter quarters for several travelling shows. This was also an important horse-breeding and flat racing country, Durham and North Yorkshire being a congenial stamping ground for travellers of all types and descriptions. Howcroft was one of the great builders and designers of this area, remaining in business making and repairing vans, especially Burton types, until just before the Second World War.

In the north-west the most popular van builders were Tongs of Kearsley near Bolton, who built many vehicles for the renowned Boswell family of gypsies, ending a van-making business, which had spanned at least five generations, with a palatial motor caravan for Emperor Bos, then head of the clan, during the late 1920s.

The two best known firms in Yorkshire were Wright of Leeds and Hill of Swinefleet, on the borders of Yorkshire and Lincolnshire (now in Humberside). Wright made all types of vehicle but later specialised in the bow top, which he may have invented or at least helped to establish. There are fine examples of his work preserved in the Castle Museum, York. Both Wright and Hill catered mainly for gypsies. Hill was a master painter of living vans and despite injuries to his right hand and arm specialised in decorative scrollwork on the ceilings of vans. He did restoration work and other forms of decorative painting until the 1960s, when he was over seventy years old, having started work in 1910 as an apprentice and serving in the First World War.

The average gypsy van cost between £40 and £150 although specials for showmen cost well over £1,000, much depending on materials and fittings chosen. The ideal of the gypsy king or queen was almost to smother the van in gold leaf, which added greatly to the cost, although few could have afforded as much of this as they would have liked. The average time needed to build a living van of the better sort was about six months. Some gypsies, however, could botch up a van of sorts, known as a *peg knife van* or wagon, in less than a day, between dawn and sunset.

8. Travelling

While on the move gypsies or showmen either led their horses or more frequently drove from the nearside of the porch or footboard. In this position they could easily reach the brake, nearly always on the left or nearside, and were better able to pull into the kerb or verge and dismount on that side, if need arose. Some also drove from the kerb or verge on a long rein.

The journey was taken in easy stages at a steady walking pace, not too fast as young foals and even goats were often following, while children enjoyed scuffling in the dust at the rear even more than riding on the van. 20 miles (32 km) was the usual target set for a day's travel, but often much shorter distances. Some travellers are known to have made up to 50 or 60 miles (80–96 km) in a day, but this would be unusual and hard on the horses. Those wishing to make a much quicker journey would break out the two-wheeled flat cart, or sometimes a light gig kept for the purpose, and drive ahead. Such vehicles were sometimes towed at the rear of a van with shafts raised, almost like a pram or tender towed in the wake of a sailing barge.

One of the great difficulties of a journey was encountering steep hills and gradients. Those that were not too long or slippery could be charged by making a flying start, with a good turn of speed, before the gradient rose too steeply, the horse urged on with cheerful encouragement so that it almost reached the summit before noticing the extra pull at the rear. Great care had to be taken not to stop, slow down or try to restart a heavy van only halfway up the hill. If failing to reach the summit in one attempt it was better to return to the bottom and start again. Long steep hills frequently needed a second horse or *sider*, harnessed to the spreader. This was not an ideal haulage position, mainly used for breaking young horses, but helped to share the load. On some ascending gradients the van would be zigzagged from side to side, pushed from the rear by women and children, but this could only be done on almost traffic-free roads. The last time the author saw this done was on the outskirts of Mountain Ash in South Wales during the early 1950s. Going downhill the wheels could be held on the drag shoe, but the older children and anyone else available also helped to hold back the load with check ropes or by bearing on the wheel tyres with metal objects.

In later years leading the horse for any distance was frowned on by the authorities, as was driving from the roadside, as sitting on the van was considered much safer. It was, however, necessary to lead the horse in the crowded conditions of a camp site, showground or race track, while many preferred to drive from the side on long reins, especially on country roads. Although many gypsies carried a coach or carriage whip with a brass-mounted stock, this was mainly for show and to make road signals.

TRAVELLING

Travelling or even starting the journey often depended on weather conditions or the state of the traffic, although a showman or huckster eager to secure a good pitch and depending on being in certain places at certain times would have to risk everything to keep his schedules. Gypsies were less restricted by a regular work pattern or timetable and could please themselves. The head of the family would be the first up and about in the morning. His first duty would be to take a look round and check on the condition of his stock and property. He would then kindle the stove or outside fire, with the aid of a few dry sticks kept for the purpose. Next he would make tea for himself and the others, rousing the rest of the family by turn. There would be a short or snack breakfast, although with plenty of hot, sweet tea to start the day. Showmen usually fared better than gypsies in this respect and frequently partook of a full English breakfast with fried or grilled food such as bacon, ham, fried bread, eggs or mushrooms.

Among English gypsies, especially in later years, the family group was usually small, while in European countries a whole tribe would move or halt together, keeping close company for many years at a time. The increase of road traffic in Britain at an earlier period may have influenced this, as well as the rapidly decreasing number of large camp sites.

Beds were made by the wife and daughters, who also dismantled the oil lamps for greater safety on the road. Anything fragile or valuable was stored away or made fully secure, sometimes wrapped between spare blankets. Tents, canopies and side sheets were then taken down and placed in the van or on a cart reserved for this purpose. Unscoured and battered pans were placed in the rearward pan box although better pans were polished and left on display near the stove. Any wandering fowl were rounded up and placed in the side (spindle) cage or pan box, on a bed of hay or straw. Those left behind were always sure to follow, half running, half flying and taking short cuts through hedges or open fields. Dogs, used either as lurchers for poaching, hare coursing or as family pets and guard dogs, were tied to the rear part of the van, under the cratch, but frequently trotting between the hind wheels of their own accord. Most livestock seemed devoted to their mobile home, despite the indignities to which they might be subjected.

While things were being cleared up in and around the van, the father and eldest son would fetch the van horse from its grazing patch and give it a good rub down or strapping. The steps of the van were then unhooked and hung under the cratch. The horse, now fully dressed or harnessed, would then be backed between the lowered shafts.

A responsible traveller always stamped out his fire before leaving and cleared up his litter. Some gypsies left a roadside message, in the form of bent twigs or cut sods, to indicate their route and direction of travel, a patteran to be interpreted by friends and followers.

There was usually a midday halt, about 12.30, of two hours or two hours and a half, with the horses unhitched and fed. They were often watered on the road before meals, using any brook, pond or public water trough available.

Towards dusk a camp was pitched, lamps and stove were relit, valuables unpacked and an evening dinner, the main meal of the day, cooked by the women of the family. Horses were staked out by the roadside or on common land, secured by 30 foot (9 m) chains. After the meal, usually a stew or meat and onions cooked together in the bucket-handled pan, there might be conversation round the fire; in later years music or the nine o'clock news on a portable radio would be the chief form of relaxation. Some members of the family might dress in their best clothes and go to a village pub or even visit local cinemas and dance halls. Unlike the canal boaters, they were rarely shy in company different from their own and, despite a mixed reception in some areas, sported a refreshing self-confidence and assurance of their own worth.

Many of the better-off gypsies and showmen had special winter quarters and spent the worst months of the year in a sheltered market place or inn yard, very often on the outskirts of a town.

The pitch or encampment of travellers on the road was known as the *atching place*, ideally a flat but sheltered ground with grazing for livestock and near a spring or running water.

9. Horses and harness

The horses used by gypsies and other travellers for pulling their vans should not be confused with the animals in which they often traded and which came from a variety of backgrounds and were destined for a wide range of purposes from the circus ring to the knacker's yard. While the showman and huckster preferred a more stolid and down-to-earth horse, the gypsy always liked a showy animal, frequently in odd colours, these being a piebald or black and white animal or a brown and white skewbald. This added a touch of gaiety to life and marked the gypsy as a person of character, little impressed by the standards of other men. Most people owning or breeding horses disliked mixed colours, which were discouraged by the breed societies. While both types were frequently of good conformation, the piebald was usually the better of the two and the more reliable. Skewbalds had a reputation for uncertain temper, although gypsies were frequently renowned for being able to train or charm vicious animals where others failed. Van horses that had been in the same family for a number of years were as safe and friendly as family pets. Young children could crawl between their iron-shod hoofs without risk of harm, while most were not troubled by traffic, and noisy crowds, hooting cars and barking dogs held few terrors for them. Often grazing along the hedgerows and verges rather than in enclosed fields, the horses of travellers had a better chance to vary their diets, guided to the right food by instinct, and this may have affected their health and temperament as much as human training.

The average gypsy van horse was a heavyweight cob or vanner, frequently a mare, for which gypsies seemed to have a special liking. Most of the London buses were formerly pulled by mares, many imported from Ireland. Treated in the right way, a mare usually showed great willingness and perseverance, understanding the nature of her work and responding well to the driver or person in charge. The cob was a dual-purpose animal, useful for both driving or riding, with a sturdy body but fairly short legs, between horse and pony. Those kept by gypsies were about 14 hands high. 1 hand is 4 inches (102 mm), or the width of the average man's hand. Vanners were slightly taller at the withers (shoulders) by a hand or so, being halfway between a cob and a Shire-type draught horse. These were sometimes known as 'half-legged' horses because their limbs were longer and sturdier than those of a cob, with a greater amount of feather or fetlock at the heels. This was often a matter of individual type as some vanners were almost clean-limbed while others were like miniature carthorses, having nearly as much feather as the Shire or Clydesdale, breeds noted for this feature. A light horse or pony was often kept for harnessing to the flat cart, gig or trap, which would be used for driving ahead of the van or taking the wife and children to the nearest town for shopping. The trap horse or pony might have a touch of hackney blood with high-stepping showy paces, its neck well arched and having a small, well set-on head.

Most gypsies preferred to see their horses with flowing manes and tails, disliking the once prevalent fashion for hogging (cutting the mane very short) and docking or shortening the tail. Docking is now forbidden by law as the full tail is useful as a fly swish, especially on hot days, flies swarming round the hind quarters of a tail-less horse causing great discomfort, if not suffering. The fore part of the horse's body is under the control of fly muscles that could be twitched, but the rear parts were beyond this protection. It was claimed by many non-gypsy drivers that a horse might get its long tail caught in the reins and thus gain control, so most draught horses were docked as a precaution against this happening. As the flowing mane did not seem right without a flowing tail the mane was cut back or hogged, at the same time as the docking took place.

The harness of van horses was a version of the average single strap harness, suitable for pulling vans, cabs and light carts. Reins, however, were very long – at least 14 feet (4.27 m) – and could be used either for driving from the front porch of the van or from the road. Harness mountings were of brass or white metal but usually the former, with hanging pendants of morocco or red patent

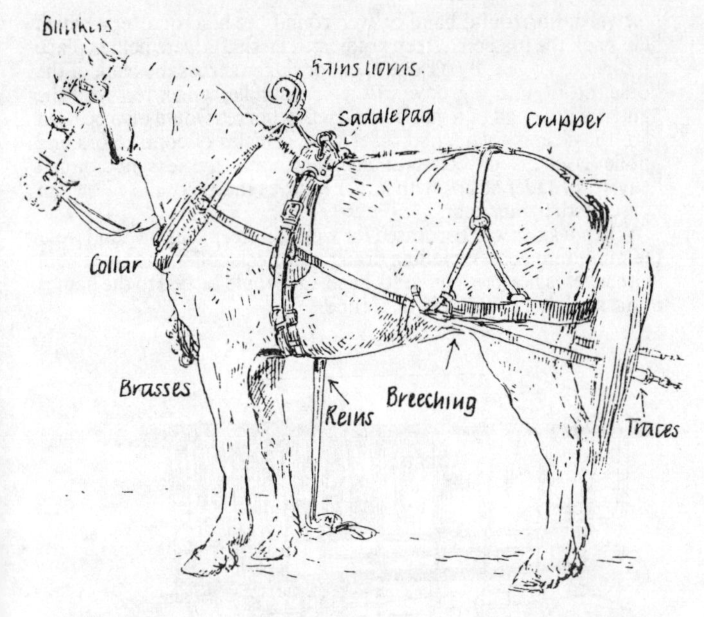

29. Horse and van harness.

leather. The bit used was of a double-ring snaffle type, while the brass-coated steel bars or hames of the neck collar, to which the tug hooks and rein rings were connected, often had a decorative curl at the terminations known as a ram's horn. Most of the harness was loaded with decorative brasses, thought to be of pagan origin, to bring good luck and ward off the evil eye.

Showmen with larger vehicles preferred Shire-type draught horses, although not always of pure breed. These were up to 18 hands high and weighed nearly a ton each. When pairs were needed for a heavy van they were usually harnessed to a centre pole but sometimes in double shafts, which resembled pairs of single shafts side by side. Additional horses, if these were needed, would be harnessed in turn to wooden draught bars or swingletrees attached to the head of the draught pole. Lord George Sanger and a few other showmen used heavy horses three abreast between two draught poles, similar to the harness and draught gear used on the first London buses introduced by George Shillibeer in 1829. Harness for such animals in heavy rigs was more than leather straps and included a high proportion of chains, as connections between poles, shafts, collars and breeching. Breeching was a rearward, horizontal band or web round the hind quarters, which held back the load on a steep gradient. The shafts were held in place on this heavy gear by a ridge chain or ridger across the back of the horse, fitting into a groove of the cart saddle, which replaced the lighter saddle pad of a van horse. Heavy horses would also be used with the sleeping vans and other road vehicles of contractors and public councils or corporations. Carthorse harness had much heavier, broader straps with larger buckles than those used on van horses with lighter gear.

When a sider was harnessed for work on steep hills it would wear the minimum gear, including draught or neck collar and traces but neither reins nor breeching. Its headstall would be tied to the hames of the shaft horse by a length of rope.

30. American gypsy van, c 1890.

10. European and American vans

The wagons and vans of showmen were very similar on both sides of the English Channel, although gypsy caravans tended to be more elegant in Britain than in continental countries. From the mid nineteenth century onwards British designs and craftsmanship, especially for everyday practical vehicles, tended to predominate. This reflected the higher standards of living and national stability in the British Isles than elsewhere, at least from the conclusion of the Napoleonic wars to the end of the century. Even today, at public auctions, British designed and constructed vehicles usually command higher prices than their equivalents from overseas.

French living vans, some of which are still used in Brittany and other parts for holiday touring, tend to have larger wheels and a proportionally longer wheelbase than British types. French vehicles are both straight and ledge sided but have panelled sides rather than matchboarding. Caravans are known to have been used in Germany and other parts of central Europe, where a long low-slung wagon appears to have been popular, drawn by a pair of horses harnessed to a centre pole. There are few records of these as it was in Germany that travelling people were often the most harassed and persecuted. In other parts of Europe, where gypsies were better tolerated, they tended to become settled communities and to give up their roving habits, along with their mobile homes. In Spain and Portugal some gypsies travelled in two-wheeled caravans, sometimes drawn by oxen.

A number of gypsies crossed the North Atlantic during the eighteenth and nineteenth centuries, continuing their wandering life in the states of New England, the Middle States and along the Atlantic seaboard. Their vans may have been adapted, in some cases, from contemporary farm vehicles and commercial wagons, in much the same way as open lots were converted from ordinary vans and drays.

One of the exhibits in the horse-drawn section of the Henry Ford Museum at Dearborn, Michigan, USA, is catalogued as a 'gypsy wagon' and dated at approximately 1895. It was discovered in 1910 at a carriage repository in Geneva, New York State, where it appears to have been abandoned, perhaps unsaleable. It was built for the King of the American Gypsies, touring in an area south and east of the Great Lakes, by whom it was part-exchanged for a horseless carriage and possibly a trailer van. Like the missionary van, it has a large front porch or platform with a raised footboard or dashboard, mounted from a sideways position through the porch. It has a ledge-type structure with overhang above the wheels and deeply recessed panelling, but far less carving and ornamentation than on British types. Some of the panels above the overhang had a number of landscape paintings or pictures of still life (fruit and flowers). There were also two large portraits of ladies in eighteenth-century costume, one each side of the small side windows. Brackets support the outer ledge, while a canopy roof protects the front porch. Suspension, with both sideways and crosswise (elliptical) springs, above the turntable, was very similar to that of the 'T' Model Ford of the 1920s. The rear carriage also had both cross and sideways springing.

An American gypsy van in the Stony Brook Museum, Long Island, New York, has elaborate panels and paintings on the front porch. Windows on either side of the doorway are of the Gothic or lancet type, deeply recessed and with glass panes bevelled along the edges.

Modern horse-drawn caravans for holidays in the west and south of Ireland, approved and checked by a government department, are versions of the bow top mounted on motorcar wheels with pneumatic tyres. Most of these have berths for four people, with adequate cooking facilities. Those hiring such vans are given a brief course of instruction on harnessing and looking after the horse, which has been specially trained and selected for the use of novices.

Bibliography

Borrow, George. *Lavengro*. 1851.
The Romany Rye. 1857.
Wild Wales. 1862.
Bostock, E. H. *Menageries, Circuses and Theatres*. 1927.
Braithwaite, D. *Fairground Architecture*. 1968.
Disher, M. W. *The Greatest Show on Earth*. 1937.
Jones, M. Article in *Heavy Horse and Driving*, summer 1978.
Parry, D. *English Horse-drawn Vehicles*. 1979.
Sanger, G. *Seventy Years a Showman*. 1926.
Simson, W. A. *History of the Gypsies*. 1865.
Smith, D. J. *Discovering Horse-drawn Commercial Vehicles*. 1977.
Smith, D. J. *Collecting and Restoring Horse Drawn Vehicles*. 1981.
Smith, R. (Gypsy Smith). *His Life and Work by Himself*. 1904.
Stables, Dr W. G. *Cruise of the Land Yacht Wanderer*. 1894.
Stone, J. H. *Caravanning and Camping Out*. 1912.
Thompson, J. *Making a Model of a Gypsy Caravan*. 1976.
Tyrwhitt-Drake, Sir G. *The English Circus and Fairground*. 1946.
Vesey-Fitzgerald, B. *The Gypsies of Britain*. 1944/46.
Ward-Jackson and Harvey, D. E. *The English Caravan*. 1972.

Places to visit

Horse-drawn caravans or items of similar interest can be seen at many museums, including those listed below. Before making a special journey, readers are advised to contact the museum to check on opening times and to establish that the items of interest will be on display when they make their visit.

Belfast Transport Museum, Witham Street, Newtownards Road, Belfast. Telephone: Belfast (0232) 51519.

Bristol Industrial Museum, Prince's Wharf, Bristol. Telephone: Bristol (0272) 299771 extension 290. (The caravan *Wanderer*.)

Hereford and Worcester County Museum, Hartlebury Castle, near Kidderminster. Telephone: Hartlebury (029 96) 416.

Hollycombe Steam Collection, Hollycombe House, Liphook, Hampshire. Telephone: Liphook (0428) 723233. (Vans used by showmen.)

Iveagh Bequest, Kenwood House, Hampstead, London NW3. Telephone: 01-348 1286.

Mary Arden Museum, Wilmcote, Stratford-upon-Avon. Telephone: Stratford-upon-Avon (0789) 3455.

Museum of East Anglian Life, Abbot's Hall, Stowmarket, Suffolk. Telephone: Stowmarket (044 92) 2229.

Reading Museum and Art Gallery, Blagrave Street, Reading. Telephone: Reading (0734) 55911 extension 2242.

West Yorkshire Folk Museum, Shibden Hall, Shibden Park, Halifax. Telephone: Halifax (0422) 52246.

York Castle Museum, Tower Street, York. Telephone: York (0904) 53611.

Yorkshire Museum of Carriages and Horse-drawn Vehicles, York Mills, Aysgarth Falls, North Yorkshire.

Index